The Christian Girl's
Guide to
Being Your Best

LEGACY PRESS®

The Christian Girl's Guide to Being Your Best

Katrina Cassel

To my sweet daughter Jessica,
May you always be successful in God's eyes.

A special thanks to Teresa C. for all your time in reading
and making suggestions to drafts of this book.

THE CHRISTIAN GIRL'S GUIDE TO BEING YOUR BEST
©2007 by Katrina Cassel, eleventh printing
ISBN 10: 1-58411-035-X
ISBN 13: 978-1-58411-035- 4
Legacy reorder# LP48211

Legacy Press
P.O. Box 70130
Richmond, VA 23255

Illustrator: Theresa Seelye

Scriptures are from the *Holy Bible: New International Version* (North American Edition), ©1973, 1978, 1984 by the International Bible Society. Used by permission of Zondervan Bible Publishers.

Printed in the United States of America

 # Contents

Hi!

Welcome to *The Christian Girl's Guide to Being Your Best.* This book is especially for girls like you.

In this book you'll learn how to be successful. No, not successful like a movie star or a famous athlete (although maybe one day you will be one of those!). Here you'll find out how to be your best in God's eyes. That's what's most important.

You might think that to be your best you have to be beautiful, or talented, or have a lot of friends or money. That is how many people judge success, but not God. He knows your talents and abilities and He wants you to use those for Him, for others and for yourself. When you are at your best in God's eyes, you are living a wonderful and happy life.

This book will guide you through many topics and activities to help you learn to be the best Christian girl you can be. Each chapter has a **Value** or principle to live by. There is a **memory verse**, too. In each chapter you will read **stories** about girls your age. Sometimes you will be asked to **write the ending** to the story or to **write a new ending** to help the girls in the stories make better choices. You'll also find different kinds of **quizzes** and **activities** for you to do. You might want to have a friend do some of the stories, quizzes and crafts with you. It's more fun to be two than one!

The things you learn in this book will help you now with school, friends and family relationships. These values will also help you later as you go to college, get a job or get married. So let's get started on your way to being your best!

Trust in the Lord with all your heart and lean not on your own understanding; in all your ways acknowledge him, and he will make your paths straight.

~ Proverbs 3:5-6

Jenna sat beside her parents in the high school gymnasium watching her brother Luke play in the basketball finals. It was a close game with lots of action, but Jenna's mind wasn't on the game itself. She was watching the cheerleaders; especially a girl named Lisa.

Lisa occasionally baby-sat for Jenna when Jenna's parents were going to be out too late for her to be alone. Jenna looked forward to those nights because Lisa was a lot of fun to be with and she always had lots of ideas for things to do when they were together. Jenna thought Lisa was the prettiest of all the cheerleaders. Plus Lisa was always on the honor roll and she sang solos at their church.

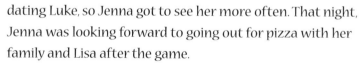

Best of all, Lisa was now dating Luke, so Jenna got to see her more often. That night, Jenna was looking forward to going out for pizza with her family and Lisa after the game.

In the last quarter, Luke scored six points and his team took the lead. When the final buzzer went off, Luke's team had won 88-84! Jenna cheered with everyone else, then she went to the car to wait for the others.

As Lisa approached the car, Jenna said, "I hope I am just like you when I get to high school!"

"Why?" Lisa asked as she tossed her pom-poms into the car trunk.

"Because you're pretty, smart, talented and the best cheerleader," Jenna answered.

Lisa laughed. "Thanks for saying that, but I really just try to do the best I can with what I have."

"What do you mean?" Jenna asked.

"Well, if you do the best you can with what you have for God and for others and for yourself," Lisa answered, "you'll be successful no matter what you do. That's a lesson my grandmother taught me. I've never forgotten it."

"But what if I do my best, and it just isn't good enough?" Jenna asked. "That wouldn't make me very successful."

"But it would make you successful in God's eyes," Lisa said, climbing into the backseat. "He doesn't judge you by your looks or talents or by how smart you are. He knows what your best is and that's all He wants from you."

Lisa scooted to the middle of the seat as Luke and Jenna got in on either side. "My favorite Bible verse is Proverbs 3:5-6," Lisa continued. "It says to trust in the Lord with all your heart, don't depend on your own understanding and remember the Lord in everything you do. Then He will give you success."

"I like that," Jenna said. "Maybe I should memorize the verses so I'll remember them when I'm not feeling good about myself."

"I'll help you with that later," said Lisa as Jenna's dad swung the car into their favorite pizza place. "But right now I want to 'be my best' at devouring a few slices of pizza!"

WHAT IS SUCCESS?

Lisa gave Jenna a good definition of what success is: doing the best you can with what you have for God, others and yourself. To be successful in God's eyes, you don't have to be beautiful, have a lot of money or possessions, be a genius or even be popular. And you don't have to be an adult to be successful. You can be a success for God right now, whatever age you are.

LiFE QUiZ! Take this quiz to see if you're on your way to success. Just circle the answer that fits you best, then score yourself at the end.

1. Your teacher announces an upcoming science fair. You are required to make a project and submit it. Science isn't your favorite subject, but you know you have to do the project so you: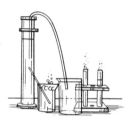

   a. Mumble and complain until your dad does it for you.

   b. Decide that as long as you have to do it you might as well find a project you like and give it your best.

   c. Just do it and get it over with.

2. Just as you sit down to watch your favorite TV show your mom asks you to peel some carrots to help with dinner. You:

   a. Turn off the television, go peel the carrots and then ask if there is anything else you can do to help.

   b. Peel the carrots as fast as you can so you don't miss much of your program.

   c. Yell, "It's not fair. I never get to watch TV."

11

3. After you rake your own lawn, your mom asks you to rake your elderly neighbor's lawn. You are tired of raking. You:

a. Rake enough to make it look like you raked.

b. Cheerfully rake up all the leaves.

c. Moan and groan until your mom does it herself.

4. Your mom asks you to clean your room. You see that some of your clothes are thrown over a chair, old test papers are scattered under your desk and you left some books from a research paper piled on the floor. You:

a. Put each item neatly where it goes.

b. Push everything under the bed so your room looks neat enough to please your mom.

c. Push everything into the closet because nothing more will fit under your bed!

5. Your teacher says that your class is going to have a talent show. Other classes will be invited to attend. He says everyone must be involved. You:

a. Decide to memorize the shortest poem you can find and recite it.

b. Plan to be sick that day.

c. Decide to use your writing talent to write something that would be both funny and informative.

Score yourself and see how you did!

1. a. 0 points for using a bad attitude to get out of a job.

b. 3 points for doing your best whether you like it or not.

c. 1 point because you did it, but not willingly or with a good attitude.

2. a. 3 points for doing the job willingly.

b. 1 point because you did the job but did just what you had to and not willingly.

c. 0 points for a bad attitude.

3. a. 1 point for doing just what you had to do.

b. 3 points because you gave it your best.

c. 0 points for a bad attitude.

4. a. 3 points for doing the job right.

b. and c. 0 points for cheating!

5. a. 1 point for at least doing that much.

b. 0 points for not trying.

c. 3 points for using your talents.

Add up your points.

Total: ___11 points___

How did you do?

If you scored 10 or above, good for you! If you want to be a Christian girl at her best, you will use your talents, work hard even when you don't feel like it and always give 100 percent.

Does that sound difficult? It doesn't have to be. And when

you stop to think about it, there are lots of ways to use the talents and abilities God has given you. If your score was less than 10, stop now and say a short prayer. God will help you do better!

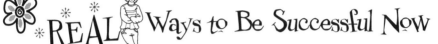

REAL Girls — Ways to Be Successful Now

Not every girl is a "Lisa" — popular, pretty and smart. After all, God makes each girl different, with her own unique qualities. But any girl can be successful by being the best she can be for God. Read on to see how some ordinary girls are becoming successful in their own ways.

Nikki M. is from Omaha, Nebraska. She loves to sing. Someday, she hopes to be a professional singer, but for now she helps direct the preschool children's choir at her church. She wrote a Christmas play for the kids to perform at the Christmas Eve service.

Lauren A. wants to be a writer. She uses her computer talents to create a newsletter for the primary-age kids at her church in Athens, Georgia. Each newsletter has a

Bible story, a puzzle and an activity that the kids can do while they're waiting for church to start.

Amanda L. is an "A" student at her middle school in Bristol, Virginia. She shares her smarts by helping other students with their homework during study period. Amanda's teacher is so impressed with the class's improved grades that she has encouraged Amanda to think about being a teacher herself when she's older.

Gretchen F. loves horses. On Saturdays, she rides in shows near her home in Green River, Wyoming. Other days, Gretchen shares her talent by helping with a horse-riding program for disabled kids. Some of them even attend her shows.

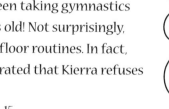

Lindsay L. is on the YMCA swim team in Walla Walla, Washington. She often wins her races. When Lindsay wins, she stops to give God the glory for giving her a strong body. If she doesn't win, she happily congratulates the swimmer who does.

A successful Christian girl finds out what her talent is and uses it for God, others and herself. Are you thinking you don't have any talents to use for God like these girls do? Be sure to read the next chapter! You'll find out that everyone has talents and abilities.

Read the following story and see if you can help Kierra find a way to use her talents and be successful in God's eyes.

Kierra sat on her bed, her heart full of discouragement. Unlike most girls, she cannot turn on a CD or tape player and listen to music to cheer herself up. Kierra has been deaf for four years, since she was 8 years old.

Kierra had already learned to talk before she became deaf, so she can communicate with others by speaking to them and then reading their lips. But she misses being able to sit down and whisper with her friends at lunch, listen to her favorite songs or hear nature sounds.

But Kierra can do something that doesn't require hearing: gymnastics. She has been taking gymnastics classes since she was four years old! Not surprisingly, Kierra is really good at bar and floor routines. In fact, her gymnastics teacher is frustrated that Kierra refuses to join the competition team. Instead, she only performs in shows the gym holds twice a year for parents.

Kierra likes helping with the toddler children's church program. She reads stories, talks to the kids and holds them on her lap. But she wishes she could hear them sing. Just today, one of the kids got angry and cried when Kierra couldn't listen to a tape and sing along with him. He didn't understand that she is deaf. Kierra almost cried, too!

Sitting on her bed thinking back on her day, Kierra wonders if she'll ever be successful at anything.

What encouragement would you give Kierra?

Even if your deaf you can make a big improvment.

How can she be her best now?

Kierra can be her best now by helping or doing things to help for children if their deaf.

How can she be successful when she's an adult?

Kierra can be successful when she is a adult by helping people that can't speak. speak learn how to

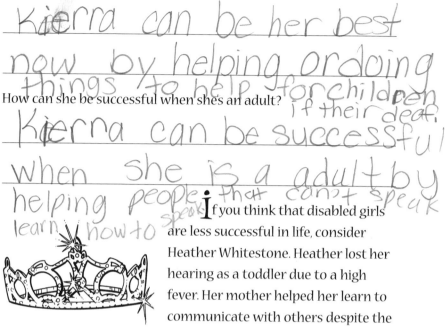

If you think that disabled girls are less successful in life, consider Heather Whitestone. Heather lost her hearing as a toddler due to a high fever. Her mother helped her learn to communicate with others despite the hearing loss. She also enrolled Heather in ballet when Heather was 5 years old. In spite of the obstacles, Heather pushed on. In 1994, she competed in the Miss America pageant, where she used her ballet training for the talent competition. Heather danced perfect pirouettes and arabesques to a Christian song by counting out the moves in her mind. She won! The following year, Heather traveled around the country as Miss America, challenging others to use their talents and abilities. She also shared her faith in God.

WRAPPING IT UP

You can begin to be a success today. Start using what you have for God, others and yourself. Do your best in everything you do. Don't forget to ask God for His help in knowing what to do.

The following chapters will give you more keys to being your best. Read each chapter and think about what it says. Enjoy the stories, answer the questions, memorize the key verses and keep a journal if you want to.

Memory Verse

Before you go any further, stop and write the memory verse for this chapter below. Memorize it. Think of it often throughout the day!

Trust in the lord with all your heart. And do not lean on your own understanding. In all your ways acknowledge Him. And he will make your paths straight.

Jot it Down

Think about a person you know who does his or her best. Write about that person here.

When I was in second grade someone named Mike had downsindrom. He did his best by not giving up and trying the hard to do what he can when he has downsindrum.

How can you be successful today?

_____

_____

Keys to Success Wall Hanging

The next chapters in this book deal with keys for your success. These keys aren't the kind you use to get in your front door — they are principles that will help you grow as a Christian girl and woman. This craft will help you remember the keys to success. As you see it hanging in your room each day, stop to think about how you are practicing those keys.

What You Need

- ✳ inexpensive craft chalkboard
- ✳ paint and paintbrush or self-stick letters
- ✳ key pattern on page 21
- ✳ stickers or other decorations
- ✳ six small, brass cup hooks
- ✳ poster board in your favorite color
- ✳ 12" ribbon
- ✳ two tacks

What to Do

1. Write or stick letters on the chalkboard that say "Keys to Success."

2. Use the key pattern to trace and cut 11 keys from poster board.

3. Write one tip on each key:
   * Be Your Best
   * Do Your Best

   * Stand Up for Yourself and What's Right
   * Set Priorities
   * Walk with God
   * Cherish Your Family
   * Value Your Integrity
   * Be Compassionate
   * Be Content
   * Persevere
   * Guard Your Tongue

Tiny Tip! Ever feel like a failure? Remember that God thinks you are a success if you do your best for Him!

4. Ask an adult to help you screw the hooks evenly-spaced along the bottom of the board.

5. Hang two keys on each hook.

6. Decorate the sides of the chalkboard with stickers or paint.

7. Attach the ribbon at the top corners of the board by using tacks.

8. Find a good spot for your Keys to Success Wall Hanging in your room.

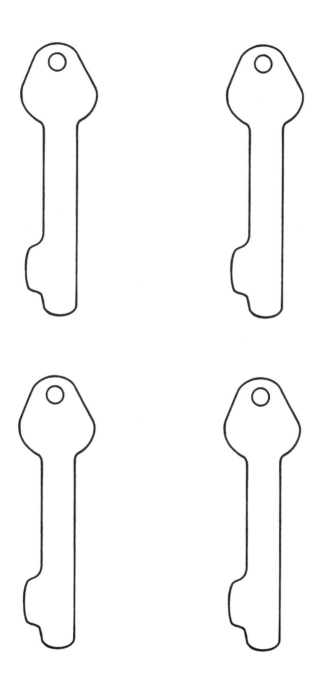

Use your talents.

I praise you because I am fearfully and wonderfully made; your works are wonderful, I know that full well.

~ Psalm 139:14

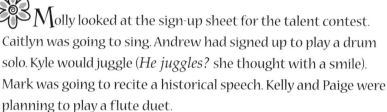Molly looked at the sign-up sheet for the talent contest. Caitlyn was going to sing. Andrew had signed up to play a drum solo. Kyle would juggle (*He juggles?* she thought with a smile). Mark was going to recite a historical speech. Kelly and Paige were planning to play a flute duet.

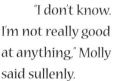

"What are you going to do for the talent contest?" Kelly asked Molly.

"I don't know. I'm not really good at anything," Molly said sullenly.

"You're good at lots of things," Kelly said. "You are the best math student in sixth grade. Besides that, you're friendly to everyone. You have more friends than anyone else."

Talent Show

Caitlyn- sing
Andrew- play drum solo
Kyle- juggle
Mark - recite historical speech
Kelly/Paige - flute duet

"Yeah, but I can't do math facts in the talent show. And being friendly isn't really a talent either; it's just the way I am. I don't have any talents," Molly insisted.

"Math and friendliness are just as important as singing or

juggling or playing an instrument, even if you can't do them on stage. Everyone has talents," Kelly said, "And yours are just as important as anyone else's. Just wait until time for the city math contest."

"I guess you're right, but I feel left out. It seems like talents you can use in a talent show are more important," Molly said.

"No way! I think it's more important to find out what you're good at and do your best with it," Kelly explained. "For you, it's math. For me, it's playing the flute. Everybody has talents — we just have to figure out how to use them."

FINDING YOUR TALENTS

Do you know what your talents are? Or do you think that you don't do anything well? No matter what you might think, you are the person God made you to be. In this chapter's key verse, the psalmist praised God for making him in an amazing and wonderful way. That's how God made you, too.

You might think your friends have more – or better – talents than you do. Maybe you wish you had musical talent. Or you want to be athletic and you aren't. Stop wishing and wanting! Find out what your true talents are and start using them for God, for others and for yourself.

Take the quiz below to help you find out your talents. Score yourself at the end.

1. If you could do anything you wanted this Saturday, you would:

a. Read the newest book by your favorite author.

b. Write in your journal about your friends.

c. Try a new computer game.

d. Visit an art museum.

e. Try out the chemistry set you got for your birthday.

f. Play one-on-one basketball with your best friend.

g. Start a cross-stitch project.

h. Talk on the phone with your friends.

i. Listen to the newest CD by your favorite singer.

j. Read to children at the library story hour.

2. You are going to the mall. The first thing you do is:

a. Go to a bookstore to browse new books.

b. Sit on a bench and people-watch.

c. Buy a book about using math in everyday life.

d. Go to a hobby store to see what art supplies they have.

e. Buy neon stars at a science store to recreate the constellations on your bedroom ceiling.

f. Go to a sports store and try on the latest style of running shoes.

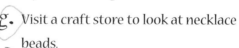

g. Visit a craft store to look at necklace beads.

h. Hang out in the food court with your friends.

i. Browse through CDs at a music store.

j. Visit a toy store and buy something for your church's nursery.

3. Your family goes to the park. You:

    a. Write a poem about what you see.

    b. Watch people talking and try to guess what they're discussing.

    c. Notice the patterns in different tree leaves.

    d. Sketch people who are sitting on a bench.

    e. Lift a rock to see what lives under it.

    f. In-line skate on a path.

    g. Look at what everyone is wearing. Design a new jogging outfit to make.

    h. Talk to the other kids who are there.

    i. Listen to a band performing there.

    j. Push little kids on swings.

4. It's time to choose a school elective. You sign up for:

    a. Journalism

    b. Social studies

    c. Computer programming

    d. Art

    e. Biology

    f. Gymnastics

    g. Family & consumer ed (home ec)

    h. Office aide

    i. Jazz band

    j. Teacher's helper in a first grade class

5. A new girl arrives at school. On the first day you:

a. Write her a letter telling her about the school.

b. Try to understand how it feels to be the new kid.

c. Ask if she needs help with her math homework.

d. Invite her to attend ceramics class with you.

e. Ask her to be your partner for an upcoming science project.

f. Ask her to go running with you after school.

g. Invite her to your house to bake cookies after school.

h. Sit with her at lunch and find out about her friends at her old school.

i. Ask her what her favorite kind of music is.

j. Offer to help her baby-sit her younger siblings.

Score yourself and see how you did!

Count how many times you circled each letter.

a's: _0_ _0_   b's: _0_

c's: _0_ _0_   d's: _0_ 2

e's: _0_ 1   f's: _0_ 1

g's: _1_ 5   h's: _2_

i's: _1_ 1   j's: _1_

Which letter did you circle most? _h's_ g's

If you circled mostly:

a's: You are strong in language and writing. You could become a writer, journalist, librarian, book reviewer, linguist or public speaker. God may use you to translate the Bible into

another language. Or you might write books and materials to help others grow as Christians. For now, join your yearbook or newspaper staff, volunteer in the library, write in a journal and create poems and stories to share with others. Join the speech or debate team if your school has one.

Tiny Tip! Don't know what your talents are even after taking the quiz? Have a friend take the quiz pretending that she is you.

b's: You have insights into your own and other people's feelings. You like to talk to others about their feelings and help them solve their problems. You will do well as a manager, principal, counselor, teacher or social worker. God may use you to counsel others, work with abused children, be an adoption counselor or go to the mission field. Continue to be helpful to your friends. When you are older, sign up to do peer counseling or help in another outreach program.

c's: You enjoy math, reason, logic and patterns. There are many jobs for you using math and computers. You may also enjoy being an accountant, bookkeeper or scientist. For now, try to use your math skills in practical ways. Figure out how to double a recipe when your parents are having dinner guests, how much fabric your mother needs to make a tablecloth, the better buy at the grocery store by looking at cost per ounce or how much gas per mile your family's car uses. God needs mathematicians with integrity to solve complex problems in the world and to develop computer technology that will help others.

d's: You enjoy art. There are many different media to explore:

oils, watercolors, pottery, ceramics, stained glass and sculpting. Try different kinds of art until you find out what you enjoy most. Once you are in high school, you will have more opportunities to take art classes. You might become an architect, graphic artist, illustrator, photographer or fashion designer. Visit your local art museum to learn more. You could use your talent to draw illustrations for Christian materials or to create artwork that would glorify God.

e's: You enjoy the **sciences.** You might be an astronomer, astronaut, biologist, zoologist, marine scientist, forest ranger, chemist, pharmacist, nurse, doctor or veterinarian, to name a few opportunities. God may use you as a doctor on the mission field or to find a cure for a disease. You might lecture about creation or write science books for Christian schools. Be sure to explore all of the different science classes as you enter high school and college.

TiNY Tip! Another way to find out your talents: List the five things you most like to do.

f's: You are an athletic person. You enjoy **sports and fitness.** You might pursue a career as a physical education teacher, recreation worker, dancer, trainer, coach or professional

athlete. As you get older, you may be able to use your skills as a junior counselor or recreational aide at Christian camps. Or, you might travel with an evangelistic sports team. As an athlete, you will be in the spotlight and others will see your Christian testimony in action.

g's: You are into **crafts, sewing and cooking.** You will enjoy family & consumer ed (home ec) class where you can experiment with different projects. You may even want to sign up for industrial arts to see what you can create with wood. Use your talents now by baking cookies for a busy mother, baking a casserole for someone in grief, mending clothes for your younger siblings, making cross stitch pictures for gifts or helping to cook your family's meals. Later, God might direct you to use these skills as part of a career as a chef or fashion designer.

h's: Making friends and **meeting new people** are fun for you. You enjoy being with others more than being alone. You are probably involved in clubs and after-school activities. People like you, who enjoy being with other people, are often elected as an officer in clubs. You will enjoy a career where you work with people. That might mean anything from being a teacher to being a social worker to managing a store. Be open to how God leads you to use your people skills.

Tiny Tip! Join a new club or activity this year. You may discover a new talent!

i's: You enjoy listening to **music** or creating music of your own. You may become a disc jockey, musician, band director, music store salesclerk, music teacher, composer or music therapist. Did you know that there are musicians who write music to take the Gospel to other countries? They compose music that appeals to the people of those countries and also teaches them about God. God also needs musicians to take His message into the world here at home.

j's: Working with children makes you happy. You like reading to them, playing with them and teaching them. You may already be using your talents as a baby-sitter. You can also be a big help in your church by assisting a busy Sunday school teacher, being a helper at vacation Bible school or working in the nursery. You could have a career as a teacher, social worker, therapist, counselor, missionary, children's author, pediatrician or even a toy designer! Use your love of children to make a difference in their lives.

USING YOUR TALENTS

The quiz helped you identify your talents and think about how you can use them. God wants us to use whatever He has given us. Do you remember Jesus' parable of the talents in

Matthew, chapter 25? The "talents" in this parable were not things like singing or writing – they were pieces of money. In the parable, a rich man was going on a

journey. Before he left, he talked to three of his servants. He gave one servant five talents, another two talents and the last one talent. The servant with five talents invested them and earned five more. The servant given two talents invested them and gained two more. But the servant who received one talent hid it in the ground. He was afraid to invest it or use it. When the rich man returned, he was very happy with the servants who had invested the money, but angry with the one who hid the money instead of using it. He took away the one talent and gave it to the servant who had 10 talents.

Why do you think Jesus told this story?

_____

Do you think Jesus was talking just about money? If not, what did he really mean?

_____

How could this story apply to you?

_____

REAL Girls

Y̱ou don't have to wait to use your talents. There are ways you can use your talents for God now – here are some examples.

Kandi S. is from Auburn, California. She loves children. She wants to be a babysitter, but she's not quite old enough yet. That doesn't stop her from being with children, though! The Murphy family, who attend Kandi's church, has children ages 5, 3, 2 and six months. Two days a week, Kandi stops at the Murphys' house on her way home from school. She plays with the children while their mother starts supper or cleans. Sometimes Kandi takes them to the small playground across the street, where Mrs. Murphy can see Kandi and the kids out her living room window. By doing this, Kandi is learning about children so she will be a better babysitter. At the same time, she is being a good Christian by unselfishly helping a busy mother.

LaTasha R., who is from Bristol, Connecticut, wants to be a writer. She writes in a journal several times a week. Every month she also writes a newsletter about what happens at her church, such as when their puppet team visited another church or the children's choir sang at a nursing home. In addition, the newsletter contains news about babies, marriages, deaths and other interesting events. LaTasha gives her newsletter to the church secretary, who types it on a computer, makes copies and sends it to all of the missionary families the church supports.

Use Your Talents.

The newsletter helps LaTasha practice her writing skills, and it helps to keep the missionaries informed of church news.

Darcy F. loves to run, and do the high jump and long jump. She is on her middle school track team in Aurora, Colorado. She practices hard and does her best

at meets. Once a year, Darcy shares her skills by coaching disabled students in track events to help them prepare for the Special Olympics. She has learned so much about disabled children and their physical abilities that she is considering a career as a special education teacher or a physical therapist when she gets older. Working with disabled kids has not only taught Darcy about her talents, it has also made her a good Christian witness of God's love for others.

Just like these three girls, you can use your talents to help others and serve God.

How can you use your talents at church?

_____

_____

How can you use your talents at school?

_____

_____

In what other ways can you use your talents?

_____

_____

Being your best means working hard to improve the talents and abilities with which God has blessed you. The more you use your God-given talents, the more talented you will become!

 # *REAL Girls* WHAT ABOUT THOSE WEAK AREAS?

Along with your strong abilities, you probably have some things you don't do so well. For example, you might be good at English but you are doing poorly in math — putting sentences together is easier for you than figuring out equations! Everyone has weak areas, so don't let them get you down. Here are some ways other girls dealt with their weak areas.

Erin M., from Lakeland, Florida, had never done well in school. She especially had trouble with spelling and handwriting. When she had to write reports, Erin often turned them in half-done, with lots of mistakes. But sixth grade turned out to be different. Erin's teacher encouraged the class to find original ways to give reports. So Erin used art, her talent, to present an oral and visual report about Abraham Lincoln by drawing four pictures about his life. Even though Erin usually had trouble speaking in front of the class, it was fun for her to describe her pictures to them. She discovered that drawing was easier than writing!

Use Your Talents.

Sara A. and Susan N. are best friends in Greenville, Alabama. Sara has always excelled in sports, but she had trouble completing

language assignments. Susan is just the opposite. She is an honor roll student but she always did poorly in physical education class. Sara and Susan made a plan to help each other. Susan tutored

Sara with her language homework, then Sara helped Susan practice the sports they played in physical education class. Plus they had fun at the same time!

Name one or two of your weak areas.

_____

Keeping in mind how the girls in the examples worked on their weaknesses, what could you do to overcome yours?

_____

_____

WRAPPING IT UP

After reading this chapter, you should know more about your abilities and talents and how you can use them for God and others. If you are still uncertain of your talents, ask your parents,

Sunday school teacher or school counselor to help you figure them out.

Memory Verse

Write the memory verse below. Memorize it so you can be reminded that God created you in a wonderful way.

_____

_____

_____

Jot It Down

What are your talents?

_____

_____

How can you use them every day?

_____

_____

How will you be able to use your talents as an adult?

_____

_____

Are You (Puzzled?) Talent Crossword

Everybody has things they do that can be used for God. The same was true in Bible times. God used people who had the desire to accomplish things for Him. Read a clue below and select which person it best describes. Fill in the names to complete the puzzle. The answers are on page 207.

Across

3. Led the Israelites out of Egypt. (Exodus 12:31-51)

4. Used an oxgoad to kill 600 Philistines. (Judges 3:31)

6. Used his strength to destroy the enemy. (Judges 16:25-30)

8. Brought others to Jesus. (John 1:40-41)

10. Shepherd, musician, king. (1 Samuel 16:23, 17:15, 28:17)

11. Followed God's orders and caused the walls to fall. (Joshua 6)

12. Used his wisdom to solve problems. (1 Kings 3:5-12)

13. During his three missionary journeys, many churches were started and the Gospel was taken to the Gentiles. (Acts 21:19)

Down

1. Preached to large crowds. (Acts 8:25)

2. Used his wealth to provide grain for the needy. (Ruth 2:8-9)

3. Chosen to be Jesus' mother. (Luke 1:26-31)

5. God made him a mighty warrior. (Judges 8:22)

7. Built an ark to save his family and the animals. (Genesis 6:13-18)

8. Took care of the first garden. (Genesis 2:15-20)

9. Made robes and clothes. (Acts 9:39)

11. Because of his planning there was plenty of grain. (Genesis 41:17-49)

Tip #2

Do your best.

Whatever you do, work at it with all your heart, as working for the Lord, not for men.

~ Colossians 3:23

Kari sat on the grass next to her Roosevelt Raiders teammates. They were all doing warm-up stretches to get ready for their track meet. It had been a good season, and the Raiders were competing in the city finals. Kari felt a knot of nervousness in her stomach as she stretched out her leg and leaned over it.

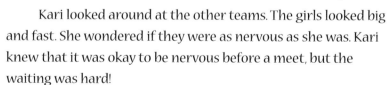

"Take a slow lap," the coach instructed. The team jogged side by side around the track in silence. Kari knew the others were as tense as she was. It was always that way before a meet! And this meet was extra important since it was the finals, and the last meet of the year.

Kari looked around at the other teams. The girls looked big and fast. She wondered if they were as nervous as she was. Kari knew that it was okay to be nervous before a meet, but the waiting was hard!

Finally, Kari's first event was announced: the 100-yard dash. Kari took her place next to the other runners. They shot out of the starting blocks as soon as the gun sounded. Kari sprinted down the lane, keeping her breathing steady and her legs and arms moving in rhythm. She felt like she was running her best, but she was still the third to cross the line.

"Good job, Kari," her coach said.

"But I only finished third," Kari said.

"You finished third, but it was your best time by two seconds," the coach told her. "You did your very best, and I'm proud of you for it."

Is everyone's "best" the same? When Kari compared herself to the other runners, she didn't feel good about her performance. Yet when her coach compared Kari's time with her other races, Kari found out she had done her very best.

It's easy to compare yourself to those who do better than you or not as well as you. But that's not what is most important. Doing your very best is what is important.

WHY?

Sometimes it's tempting to do a half-hearted job on your homework, sports team practice, science project, washing the dishes or whatever you might be doing.

 Hannah was watching her favorite television show when her mother came into the room.

 "Have you done all your homework?" her mother asked.

"Almost. I just have an English assignment left. I'll do it when this show's over," Hannah said.

 "When this show is over, it's your bedtime," her mother reminded her. "Turn the television off and do the assignment now."

 "But Mom," Hannah protested, "it's a stupid writing assignment and I don't have any ideas for it."

"You usually like to write. What's the problem with this assignment?" her mother asked.

"It's an essay on what we value most about our

country. I mean, who really sits around and thinks about that kind of stuff?" Hannah complained.

"You, for one, if you are going to get this assignment done. Surely Mrs. Friesen didn't just assign the paper today."

"No. She assigned it on Monday. I've been thinking about it, I just haven't started."

"Well, now's the time," her mom announced.

Hannah sat at the table with a pencil and paper. She wrote "What I Appreciate Most About Our Country" on the top line of the paper, then thought for a minute and scribbled down a few ideas. She stuck it in her folder so her mother wouldn't read it. Hannah knew her mother would make her redo the paper if she saw what a half-hearted job Hannah had done.

The next day, Mrs. Friesen collected all the writing assignments. Then she told the class, "This assignment is especially important. Mr. Walker, our principal, has agreed to let the middle school have its own newspaper next year. He is going to choose a student editor based on this writing assignment and writing assignments done by students in other classes. He is also going to choose student reporters to write articles for the paper. The staff list will be posted on the front bulletin board on Monday. Isn't it exciting that we get to have our own newspaper?"

Hannah slumped down in her seat. She would love to be the editor, or at least a reporter. She knew she was one of the best writers in the class, but she also knew that this assignment was the worst one she'd ever done. She wouldn't even need to check the bulletin board on Monday. Her name wouldn't be on the list.

How did Hannah feel when she heard that the principal was choosing the editor and the reporters based on the writing assignment they handed in?

_____

_____

How would Hannah have done her paper differently if she had known it would be used to choose the editor and reporters?

_____

_____

Think about a time when you handed in an assignment that wasn't your best. How did you feel when you handed it in?

Tiny Tip! Instead of making a "to do" list, make a "have done" list so you can see all you have accomplished.

_____

_____

How did you feel when you got it back?

_____

How are those feelings different from when you hand in your best work?

Hayley listened as the police officer discussed school bus safety. This was the same presentation they heard every year at her school. Hayley sighed in boredom. She was glad when it was finally time for her class to go back to their room.

"I'm handing out paper to make safety posters," said Hayley's teacher, Mrs. Decker. "I want you to think  of one bus safety rule. Write that rule neatly across the bottom of your paper. Then illustrate the rule. Do your best work."

Hayley looked at the clock. Only 45 more minutes and school would be over for the day! She couldn't wait. Her gymnastics team was performing at the PTA meeting that evening. Hayley was eager to show off all of her hard work on gymnastics.

Hayley's mind was more on somersaults than safety. She just wanted this school day to end! So she wrote "Always stay seated" across the bottom of her paper. Then she drew a quick picture of stick figures sitting on bus seats.

Hayley turned to look at her friend Bethany. She saw Bethany carefully coloring in the background of her poster. Bethany had written her safety rule in neat block letters. Hayley wondered how Bethany could concentrate on the poster — she was also on the gymnastics team performing that night.

"Okay, finish up your posters," Mrs. Decker called out. "Make sure your name is on the back and put them in a pile on my desk. I will be hanging the posters in the school lobby along with posters done by the other sixth grade classes. Tonight we will have ballots at the PTA meeting so parents can vote for the best poster. There will be prizes for the top three."

Hayley cringed. She knew she wasn't a good enough artist to win one of the prizes, but she could have done better work than she did. Hayley was embarrassed that her poster would be hanging in the lobby for everyone to see. She wished Mrs. Decker had told the class that the posters would be on display.

How do you think Hayley will feel when she sees her poster in the lobby?

_____

How will she feel when her parents see her poster?

_____

In what activities do you give your best?

_____

In what things don't you try your hardest?

_____

What would happen if you made your best effort in all of your activities?

_____

_____

Both Hannah and Hayley would have done much better jobs on their assignments if they had known how important they were. But, they should have done their best anyway. It's important to do your best in everything you do because:

 You can be proud of yourself and your work.

 You will get better at difficult tasks when you try harder to do them.

God wants us to do everything as though we were doing it for Jesus.

Let's give Hannah and Hayley another chance. This time, you write the endings of their stories.

 Hannah was watching her favorite television show when her mother came into the room.

"Have you done all your homework?" her mother asked.

"Almost. I just have an English assignment left. I'll do it when this show's over," Hannah said.

"When this show is over, it's your bedtime," her mother reminded her. "Turn the television off and do the assignment now."

"But Mom," Hannah protested, "it's a stupid writing assignment and I don't have any ideas for it."

"You usually like to write. What's the problem with this assignment?" her mother asked.

"It's an essay on what we value most about our country. I mean, who really sits around and thinks about that kind of stuff?" Hannah complained.

"You, for one, if you are going to get this assignment done. Surely Mrs. Friesen didn't just assign this paper today if it's due tomorrow."

"No. She assigned it on Monday. I've been thinking about it, I just haven't started."

"Well, now's the time," her mom announced.

Hannah sat at the table with a pencil and paper. She wrote "What I Appreciate Most About Our Country" on the top line of the paper. Hannah thought for a minute and then… (finish the story!)

_____

_____

_____

_____

_____

_____

Hayley listened as the police officer discussed school bus safety. This was the same presentation they heard every year at her school. Hayley sighed in boredom. She was glad when it was finally time for her class to go back to their room.

"I'm handing out paper to make safety posters," said Hayley's teacher, Mrs. Decker. "I want you to think of one bus safety rule. Write that rule neatly across the bottom

of your paper. Then illustrate the rule. Do your best work."

Hayley looked at the clock. Only 45 more minutes and school would be over for the day! She couldn't wait. Her gymnastics team was performing at the PTA meeting that evening. Hayley was eager to show off all of her hard work on gymnastics.

Hayley's mind was more on somersaults than safety. She just wanted this school day to end! So she wrote "Always stay seated" across the bottom of her paper, then

_____

_____

_____

_____

_____

Think About it ❓❓❓

Picture in your mind the last homework assignment that you turned in at school. Answer these questions:

Did you put the proper heading on the paper?

Yes _____ **No** _____

Did you read all of the instructions and follow them?

Yes _____ **No** _____

Did you complete every question?

Yes _____ No _____

Did you answer the questions thoroughly?

Yes _____ No _____

Did you use your best handwriting or typing?

Yes _____ No _____

Did you completely erase or delete any mistakes?

Yes _____ No _____

Was the paper neat and unrumpled when you turned it in?

Yes _____ No _____

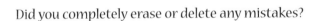

If you marked all "yes," then you did your best work. If you had one or more answers as "no", think about the work you are doing. The next time you are ready to turn in an assignment, ask yourself these questions again.

Homework isn't the only thing that deserves your best. Do your best in band, practicing piano, babysitting, doing the dishes, making your bed, performing in ballet class or in any other activity you do.

WRAPPING IT UP

It's important to do your best in everything. God requires it of you, and it's a good habit to begin today. If you do your best now, you will probably do your best in your adult life. That will help you be successful in whatever God leads you to do.

Memory Verse

Write the memory verse below. Repeat it often, especially when you are doing a task you don't like to do.

_____

_____

Jot It Down

When is it difficult for you to do your best?

_____

_____

How can you do your best when you are doing something that you don't like to do?

_____

_____

How do you feel when you do your best even though a task is difficult?

_____

_____

Secret Code

This chapter showed how important it is to try to do your best in everything. If you don't try, you might miss out on the chance to feel proud of your work!

There is a secret message in the puzzle below that will help you remember always to do your best. To decode the message, look at the first blank marked "A6." Put one finger on the A and one finger on the 6. Bring your fingers together (one finger down and the other across). Are you at W? Good, now write it on the first blank. Then figure out the next letter by putting one finger on G and another on 3. Write H on the blank. Continue until you can read this special message from God to you. (Use this tricky tactic to code messages for your friends to decode!)

	1	2	3	4	5	6
	A	Y	B	X	C	W
	T	F	U	E	V	D
	G	S	H	J	I	R
	P	O	N	M	L	K

_____ ___ ___ ___ ___ ___ ___ ___   ___ ___ ___ ___
A6 G3 A1 T1 T4 T5 T4 G6   A2 P2 T3 G6

___ ___ ___ ___   ___ ___ ___ ___ ___   ___ ___   ___ ___
G3 A1 P3 T6   T2 G5 P3 T6 G2   T1 P2   T6 P2

___ ___   ___ ___   ___ ___ ___ ___   ___ ___ ___
T6 P2   G5 T1   A6 G5 T1 G3   A1 P5 P5

___ ___ ___ ___   ___ ___ ___ ___ ___.
A2 P2 T3 G6   P4 G5 G1 G3 T1   **— Ecclesiastes 9:10**

The solution is on page 207.

Stand up for yourself and for what's right.

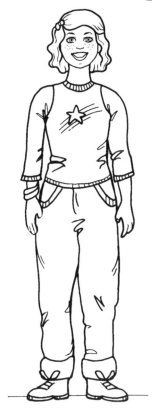

Do not be wise in your own eyes; fear the Lord and shun evil.

~ Proverbs 3:7

Brittany counted the money she had saved. She'd made $20 this month for baby-sitting, saved $10 of her allowance and received $20 for her birthday from her grandmother. Brittany knew exactly what she was going to buy with the money: books. She loved to read, and she wanted to buy a new series of books by her favorite author.

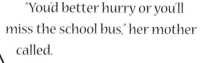

Brittany put away the money and picked up her backpack.

"You'd better hurry or you'll miss the school bus," her mother called.

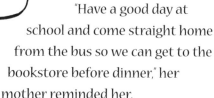

"I'm ready," Brittany said. "See you later."

"Have a good day at school and come straight home from the bus so we can get to the bookstore before dinner," her mother reminded her.

Brittany couldn't wait to see her friends and tell them about her money.

"Guess what?" she said to Kayley as she took her seat on the bus, "I have $50 and I'm going to buy a really cool set of books. You read a girl's journal and write your own entries…"

"Books!" Kayley exclaimed. "You have $50 and you're going to buy books?"

"Yeah, but not just regular books, in these you read about the life of this 12-year-old girl in the 1800s and then…"

"Megan, you won't believe this," Kayley said to the girl across the aisle, "Brittany has $50 and she's buying books!"

"No way!" Megan exclaimed.

"If I had $50 I'd buy some CDs. I'm tired of listening to my older brother's stuff," Kayley said.

"I'd get clothes," Megan said. "Books?"

"Well," Brittany said. "I could use some clothes, and I don't have any CDs. I guess I'm not really sure what I want to buy."

Do you think Brittany was telling the truth when she said she wasn't sure what she wanted to buy? No. She really wanted to buy books, but at the same time she wanted the approval of her friends. If Brittany doesn't buy the books because of what her friends said, then she is giving in to "peer pressure."

WHAT IS PEER PRESSURE?

"Peers" are the people around you who are similar to you and share common experiences. They are the other students in your class at school or your Sunday school class, or friends and acquaintances near your age. "Peer pressure" is when your peers try to get you to do something they want you to do. Peer pressure makes you imitate others instead of doing what you want. It can cause you to do things you know are wrong. Peer pressure doesn't always have to be bad, though. It can be good if you are part of a group of girls who do what is right. You can also use peer pressure to get others to join you in doing good things.

Tell about a time you faced peer pressure this week.

_____

_____

_____

Was it positive (good) peer pressure or negative (bad) peer pressure?

LiFE QUIZ! DO YOU GIVE IN?

Are you likely to be a victim of negative peer pressure? Take the quiz below to see how much you are affected by it. Circle one answer for each situation. Be honest!

1. You buy a new T-shirt. You think it's really great, but when you wear it to school your friends say it's just not cool. You:

   a. Decide you don't really like it after all.

   b. Wear it when they aren't around.

   c. Wear it to school because you like it.

2. Your teacher announces that a new club to help protect the environment is being formed. You think it sounds interesting and want to join. You ask your friends to join with you but they say it's silly. You:

   a. Decide not to join. You can recycle cans and do other environmental things on your own.

   b. Join the club, but don't mention it to your friends.

   c. Join enthusiastically.

3. A new student arrives at school. Her clothes are out of style and her hair is tangled and messy. All of the popular kids laugh at her behind her back. You:

   a. Laugh. You don't want them to think you are like her!

b. Don't laugh, but ignore the new student.

c. Offer to help the new student find her way around the school because you think she's nice.

4. You are a math whiz, and everyone knows it. The in-crowd starts asking you for answers to homework. You:

a. Give them the answers. Who will know the difference?

b. Say, "I haven't done my homework yet" even though you have.

c. Tell them you'll help them with the homework but won't do it for them.

5. Your science teacher says the Bible is "dumb." He says he thinks educated people do not accept the Bible as fact. You:

a Pretend you agree without actually saying it.

b. Don't lie, but just ignore the situation.

c. Calmly and respectfully tell your teacher what you believe.

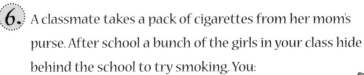

6. A classmate takes a pack of cigarettes from her mom's purse. After school a bunch of the girls in your class hide behind the school to try smoking. You:

a. Take one puff just to fit in.

b. Tell them you are allergic to cigarette smoke.

c. Tell them, "No, thanks. It's a bad habit I'd rather not start."

Count how many times you circled each letter.

a: _____

b: _____

c: _____

Mostly A's: Beware! You give in easily to others, and peer pressure controls your actions.

Mostly B's: You are wishy-washy. You don't want to give in, but at the same time you aren't ready to stand up for yourself.

Mostly C's: Good for you! You aren't afraid to follow your own feelings and conscience.

STANDING UP FOR YOURSELF

Sometimes compromise is good. Everyone has to give in at times to come up with solutions that are good for everyone. For

example, imagine that your family plans to go out to eat then rent a movie and watch it together at home. Your brother wants hamburgers, but you want pizza. You can't have both, so you compromise. You tell him you will eat hamburgers with him if you get to choose the movie. Or, he can choose the movie but you get to pick where to eat. That's a compromise because both of you get something you want.

Compromise is different than giving in to peer pressure. When you give up your own wants and desires just because others don't like what you like, you are falling prey to peer pressure. For instance, maybe all your friends decide they don't like pizza, so you give up pizza to fit in with them. It's not fair to you if you have to give up something you really like. And it's not fair to your friends because you're letting them think that you are someone you are not. You are a pizza lover disguising yourself as a pizza hater!

True friends won't pressure you to have the exact same likes and dislikes that they do. Your differences make you interesting and unique.

What can you do when your friends want you to be exactly like them? Here are some ideas:

Remember that God made everyone unique. He made us with our own likes, dislikes, talents and personalities. God wants each of us to be the best that we can be, not copies of each other.

Realize that trying to be like everyone else may make you unhappy on the inside because you aren't doing, wearing or saying the things that make you happy. What your group wants you to do is what makes them happy, not you.

Don't be afraid to be different. If you like different clothes than some of your friends do, tell them, "I like this shirt and I'm going to wear it because it looks good on me." Maybe they will even want to copy you!

Remember that true friends will accept you for who you are. They will respect your talents and tastes. If some people threaten to not be your friends because you won't copy them, maybe they really aren't good friends anyway.

DOUBLE TROUBLE

The power of peer pressure is that most people don't want to feel left out. They want to fit in and that makes them do things they wouldn't normally do. But some peer pressure goes beyond just likes and dislikes. This kind of peer pressure can get you into real trouble. Have your friends ever wanted you to go along with something that is wrong? Maybe you can relate to the girls in this story.

Kaitlyn stuffed her homework in her backpack and ran to catch up with her friends, Lindsey and Sara. "Can you believe all the homework we have tonight? I've got to get home and start on it," she said.

"Let's stop at the store on the way home," Lindsey said. "I want to get a candy bar. I've felt like eating chocolate all day. Jason was eating a Snickers at lunch, and it looked really good."

"Okay, I'll go with you, but I don't have any money," Kaitlyn said.

"That's okay, we don't either," Lindsey said.

"Then how are you going to get candy?" Kaitlyn asked.

"The same way we always do," Sara said with a laugh. "Come on."

The girls opened the door and went into the store. A sales clerk greeted them. "How can I help you?" she asked.

"I need to look at notebooks," Sara said. She followed the sales clerk to the school supply section.

While the clerk was busy showing Sara the notebooks, Lindsey grabbed a handful of candy bars and stuck them in her backpack. She grabbed another handful and handed them to Kaitlyn. "Quick! Put them in your back pack."

"I can't do that," Lindsey said.

"Oh, don't be a chicken. If you want to be friends with us, you have to take candy, too. My parents spend enough money in here to make up for it. Hurry!"

Kaitlyn unzipped the small front pouch of her backpack and stuck the candy bars in it. She swung the backpack onto her back as Sara and the sales clerk returned empty-handed.

But in her hurry, Kaitlyn had forgotten to zip the pouch on her backpack. So as she swung her backpack, Kaitlyn watched in horror as candy bars tumbled from her back onto the floor.

The sales clerk snatched them up. "You girls need to come to the office with me. This is shoplifting," she said angrily.

Kaitlyn wanted to be friends with Sara and Lindsey so she did something she knew was wrong. She got in trouble with the store manager, and then with her parents. She knew God wasn't pleased with her either.

Why do you think it was so important for Kaitlyn to have Sara and Lindsey as friends?

_____

_____

Stand Up for Yourself and for What's Right.

Do you think they were really her friends? Why or why not?

_____

_____

What could Kaitlyn have done differently?

_____

_____

_____

What can Kaitlyn do now to be sure something like this doesn't happen again?

_____

_____

TiNY Tip! Find two other girls who want to do what is right to be your encouragement buddies. Call each other when you think you might give in to peer pressure.

Wendy watched her friends climb up on the Smiths' garage roof. By standing on the trash can, they could reach the lowest branch on the tree beside the garage. From there it was easy to climb the tree and get onto the roof. Wendy wasn't sure she really wanted to do it. It looked pretty high up, and she knew the Smiths had threatened to call the police if they caught kids on their garage roof again. Her parents had also told her to stay away from the Smiths' property. They had heard about the problems neighbors were having with kids climbing onto their roofs and walking around.

"Come on," Michael called. "I didn't think you were such a baby."

"I can do it, I just don't want to do it," Wendy said.

"Yeah, sure. Chicken." Michael taunted. "Why don't you go home to your mommy?"

"Okay, I'm coming," Wendy said. It was easier than she thought to climb up the tree and onto the garage roof.

"Hey, look at me!" Michael said standing up and raising his arms in victory. "I'm king of the world."

"Sit down," Aaron said. "Someone will see you." Aaron gave Michael a push to make him sit down, but it made Michael lose his balance. He quickly sat down, but he slid down the roof and right over the edge, falling to the ground below.

Aaron and Wendy peered over the edge. "Are you okay?" Aaron asked.

"Except for my arm. It really hurts, and it's swelling fast!" Michael said. "I'd better go home."

"We'll go with you," Aaron said. "We're all in this together."

Wendy felt a knot of fear in her stomach. She knew her dad wasn't going to be happy to hear about this one!

Wendy took a risk because her friends were doing it. What do you think made her join them?

_____

_____

What could Wendy have done to avoid this situation?

_____

_____

What similar words did Lindsey (first story) and Michael (second story) say?

_____

_____

Think of something a peer asked you to do that was wrong. How did you feel?

_____

_____

Standing Up to Bad Peer Pressure

Saying no to friends or classmates isn't always easy. But God promises to help you. 1 Corinthians 10:13 says, "No temptation has seized you except what is common to man. And God is faithful; he will not let you be tempted beyond what you can bear. But when you are tempted, he will also provide a way out so that you can stand up under it."

This verse says a lot about not giving in to peer pressure. First, it explains that everyone faces these same situations. Other girls like you are tempted to shoplift, cheat on a test or be

67

cruel to another classmate just to fit in with the crowd. You aren't alone.

Second, this verse tells you that you can trust God. Sometimes your friends might fail you. Even your family might let you down. But God never will. He will be with you just as He was with Abraham, Moses, Paul and all the other men and women of the Bible He led and protected. His promises are just as true for you as they were for them.

This verse promises you that you can stand against every temptation that comes your way. But you can't do it alone, you must do it with God's help. He will provide a way out for you.

Tiny Tip! Is someone pressuring you to do wrong? Say no and ask another friend to come over after school to study or talk.

Here are some things that might help you stand against temptation:

Pray. Ask God to help you do what is right even if other people are doing wrong. Remember Shadrach, Meshach and Abednego? The king wanted them to bow down to an idol he made. They wouldn't do it. They said they couldn't bow down to anyone but the true God. They stood for the right thing even when everyone else bowed to the idol! They ended up in a fiery furnace for their choice, but God not only protected them, He used the situation to show that He really is the true God.

Talk to an adult. Discuss your concerns with an adult you trust, such as a parent, Sunday school teacher or pastor. They were all your age at one time! They may not have faced the same situation you are in, but they all faced peer pressure of some type. If you are afraid to talk to an adult because you think you might get in trouble, remember that any trouble you get in will be less than the trouble you face from giving in to peer pressure.

Take time to think. When you do something suddenly without thinking, you are acting "impulsively." Acting impulsively could get you into a lot of trouble! Take time to think about the consequences of your actions. Think about other solutions. Don't be afraid to tell your friends, "I need time to think about it."

Avoid temptation. If you know some of your friends shoplift, for example, don't go into a store with them. If you avoid bad situations, you won't feel pressured to get involved.

Look for new friends. If your "friends" are willing to let you get into trouble, they are not very good friends. It may be time to look for friends who share your values. Try making new friends in your Sunday school class, neighborhood or school.

MAKING PEER PRESSURE POSITIVE

As a Christian, not only can you avoid negative peer pressure, you can use peer pressure for good by influencing your friends to do what's right. Maybe you and your friends could decide to all get good grades, help at school or at home, do one good deed a day or spend time reading the Bible together. Here's a story about a girl who made peer pressure pretty.

Rachel was working on her homework when she heard her mom talking on the phone about some of their church's older members who lived in a nursing home.

"It's too bad they don't have any visitors," her mom said.

After her mom hung up the phone, Rachel asked, "What were you talking about?"

"Mrs. Wells and I are concerned about those two ladies from church who've been moved to nursing homes," her mom replied. "They don't ever have visitors. We're not sure if they don't have relatives in the area or if their relatives don't visit often. Either way, they are alone much of the time."

Rachel thought about what her mom had said. The next day after school she sat on her front porch talking with her friends, Shanté and Dawn.

"Let's ring doorbells and run away," Dawn suggested. "It's so funny to watch people come out and look around to see who rang the bell."

"Okay," Shanté agreed. "I'm bored anyway."

"No," Rachel said. "I don't want to do that."

"Why not?" Dawn asked. "We always do things together."

"Yeah, but that's what little kids do," Rachel said. "Let's do something more important."

"Like what?" Shanté asked.

"Well, my mom was telling me about some people in the nursing home who are lonely because they don't have any visitors," Rachel said. "Maybe we could use markers and draw them pictures or make them cards. Maybe we could even go visit them."

"Okay," Shanté said. "Yeah, you're right. That does sound like a more grown-up idea than ringing door bells. And we'd be doing something good for someone else."

Was Dawn's suggestion right or wrong? Why?

_____

_____

_____

Why was Rachel's idea better?

_____

_____

_____

What do you think would have happened if Dawn and Shanté hadn't agreed to Rachel's idea?

_____

_____

_____

WRAPPING IT UP

You've learned what peer pressure is and the difference between positive and negative peer pressure. Now it's up to you. You will face peer pressure all of your life. If you can learn to say no now and stand up for what you believe in and what's right, you will be at your best.

Memory Verse

Before going on to the next chapter, write the memory verse below. Repeat it often, especially when others are trying to get you to do something wrong.

_____

_____

Jot It Down

How does peer pressure affect you?

_____

_____

How can you and God work together to beat your peer pressure problems?

_____

_____

_____

What can you do at school, home or in your neighborhood to use positive peer pressure?

_____

_____

_____

Hanging Banner

This chapter explained how important it is for you to stand up for yourself and for what's right. When you don't stand up for those things, you aren't being true to yourself or to God. Make this banner as a daily reminder to stand up for what's right.

What You Need

* plain fabric, burlap or felt
* dowel rod
* fabric markers or paint, or felt
* glue
* 18" of yarn
* pencil

What to Do

1. Cut your fabric to be the size of banner you want. Pick any size you like! Then be sure your dowel rod is 2" longer than the width of your fabric.

2. Lightly pencil "Stand Up for What's Right" on your banner.

3. Once you have the words the way you want them to look, go over them in marker or paint, or cut the letters from felt and glue them to the fabric.

4. Trace both of your feet on the banner with a pencil (if your feet don't fit, borrow your younger brother or sister) and go over them in marker or paint; or trace your feet onto felt, cut them out and glue them on your banner.

5. Allow the banner to dry overnight.

6. Fold over 1" of the cloth on the top back of the banner.

7. Glue just the very edge, leaving a pocket. Allow to dry thoroughly.

8. Slide the dowel rod into the pocket.

9. Tie yarn to each end of the dowel rod.

10. Hang your banner in your room to remind you to stand up for yourself and what's right.

Set priorities.

> But seek first his kingdom and his righteousness, and all these things will be given to you as well.

> **~ Matthew 6:33**

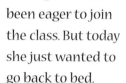

Miao lay in bed not wanting to face the day. It was Saturday, usually her favorite day. On Saturdays she went to a special class for adopted Chinese children. There they learned the Chinese language, customs, crafts and cooking. Miao enjoyed being with other adopted Chinese kids and learning new things, and she'd

been eager to join the class. But today she just wanted to go back to bed.

Lately it seemed there was always something Miao was supposed to be doing. On Mondays she had piano, on Tuesdays

ballet, on Wednesday church youth group, and on Thursdays an after-school Bible club for girls. Miao enjoyed these things, and they were all good activities, but having so many activities made it hard for her to do her best at any of them. She had homework to do, piano lessons to practice, ballet stretches and steps to perfect, projects to do for youth group, verses to learn for Bible club.

Miao rolled over and pulled the covers over her head.

Maybe I could sleep all day and no one would notice, she thought.

Miao is trying to do too much. Her activities are fine choices, but if she doesn't eliminate some of them, she is going to end up too tired to like any of her activities. Miao needs to set some priorities.

WHAT ARE PRIORITIES?

When people ask about your priorities they are asking what is most important to you. For example, Miao has a lot going on in her life. She has some activities that will make her a stronger Christian, and some activities that will improve her talents and skills. Besides that, she has responsibilities at home and schoolwork to do. Miao needs to decide which of her activities are the most important. As she chooses how to spend her time and energy, she is setting her priorities.

Getting your priorities in the right order is important if you want to be your best. If a businessman spends more time on fishing and reading magazines than on his job, he won't be doing his best at work. In the same way, if you spend more time having fun with friends than on your schoolwork, you won't be successful in school. Let's explore how to set priorities.

SETTING PRIORITIES

Sometimes adults write purpose (or "mission") statements to help them set their priorities. The statements are a sentence or two that tell what they really want to do with their lives. You don't have to be an adult to write one – you can do it now!

Here are a few girls' mission statements and why they chose them.

"To do my best in school and in my church club program."

~ Heather B., Park City, Utah

Heather's priorities are doing her homework, studying for tests, learning Bible verses for church club and completing club projects. It doesn't mean that she doesn't spend time with her friends, only that her first priorities are school and church club.

"To learn things at school and church that will help me be a missionary later."

~ **Samantha V., Salem, Oregon**

Samantha already knows she wants to be a missionary when she is older. She is interested in other countries, how

different people live and how current events affect missionaries. Sam knows she must study hard to go to college and get more Bible training. She learns all she can in Sunday school and at church along with reading the Bible and praying on her own. This doesn't mean that she can't enjoy doing things that other girls do for fun. It does mean she has an idea of what she wants to do with her life, and preparing for it is her priority.

"To find ways to serve God at home, church and school."

~ **Emily C., Columbus, Ohio**

For Emily, reaching out to others and helping when she can is a priority. She has tutored a student in math, invited friends to church, helped her teacher after school and offered to take care of her younger siblings. She finds time to have fun, but her first priority is serving.

How do you most like to spend your free time?

_____

Which activities are most important to you?

_____

Now it's your turn to write a purpose statement.

_____

_____

_____

What you wrote on these lines will help you set priorities. Of course, as a Christian, your first priority should be to "Trust in the Lord with all your heart and lean not on your own understanding; in all your ways acknowledge him, and he will make your paths straight" (Proverbs 3:5-6). Remember that Scripture from Chapter 1? But whatever you choose to do, put God first in it. As the key verse for this chapter says, "But seek first his kingdom and his righteousness, and all these things will be given to you as well" (Matthew 6:33).

God will use your interests, abilities and personality for His glory. That doesn't mean all your activities have to be church activities. You can be a witness for God in gymnastics or ballet, on the soccer field or in the classroom.

Now that you know how to set priorities, let's see if we can help Miao with her priorities.

Suppose Miao's purpose statement is "To learn more about China, and to learn more about God." Which activities would be most important to her?

_____

_____

Using Your Time

Let's look at how much free time you have and how you use it. Read through the list of activities on the next page. As you read down the list, cross out the activities you do not do. On the blank lines on page 82, add activities you do that are not listed.

Next, figure out how much time you spend on each activity. On the line before "hours" write the number of hours per day that you spend on that activity. If you don't spend a whole hour, write a fraction on the line. For example, if you read your Bible for 15 minutes per day that would be 1/4 hour.

If you do an activity only on a certain day, write the day after "hours." For example, if you have a two-hour piano lesson on Tuesdays write a 2 on the line and write "on Tuesday" after the word "hours."

How much time each day do you spend:

In school _____ hours

Watching television _____ hours

Talking on the phone _____ hours

Doing homework _____ hours

Reading your Bible _____ hours

Praying _____ hours

Doing things with your family _____ hours

Helping with jobs at home _____ hours

Spending time with friends _____ hours

Reading _____ hours

Practicing a musical instrument, dance or other skill

_____ hours

At lessons _____ hours

Working on a hobby _____ hours

In church and Sunday school _____ hours

In a church youth program _____ hours

Getting ready in the morning _____ hours

Getting ready for bed at night _____ hours

Eating meals with family _____ hours

Write activities you do that were not listed:

_____ _____ hours

_____ _____ hours

_____ _____ hours

What do you spend the most time doing other than going to school?

_____

Which things could you spend less time doing?

_____

Which things should you spend more time doing?

_____

Still unsure of how you spend your time? Grab some colored pencils or crayons and follow the instructions to fill in the time schedule on the next page.

Color blue the time you spend in school. Include the time it takes you to get to school and back home again.

Color red the times you are at church. Include the time it takes you to drive to church and get back home.

Color green anything else that happens at specific times, including lessons, clubs or sports practices.

Color orange meal times and any other family times.

Color yellow the time you spend reading the Bible and praying.

Color gray the time you spend doing jobs around the house.

Color purple the time you spend doing homework.

	Sun.	Mon.	Tues.	Wed.	Thurs.	Fri.	Sat.
6:00							
7:00							
8:00							
9:00							
10:00							
11:00							
12:00							
1:00							
2:00							
3:00							
4:00							
5:00							
6:00							
7:00							
8:00							
9:00							
10:00							

Look at your colored chart. The time you have left is when you can do whatever you want to do. This "empty" time could be when you do what you listed in your purpose statement, if you haven't listed it already.

Remember to leave time for fun. If your squares were filling up too quickly, you might be trying to do too many things. Consider giving up an activity or two so that you have more free time to do what is most important to you – and to relax!

It's All Too Much!

Tara looked at the social studies test in front of her. She couldn't answer hardly any of the questions. She had planned to study every night but she hadn't been able to.

On Sunday night she had youth group and church. On Monday and Wednesday nights she had cheerleading

practice, which was especially important because they were getting ready for the state cheerleading competition.

On Tuesday night was Girl Scouts. Tara didn't really like being in Girl Scouts but her mom had been in scouts and so had Tara's two older sisters, so she was expected to be a scout, too. Thursday night was gymnastics. She needed the gymnastics class to help her with her cheerleading skills.

Tara had tried to study in the car on the way to all her lessons and classes but it had obviously not been enough time. She was up late every night just to get her homework done, let alone trying to study for this test.

As Tara handed in the test, she knew she had failed even though her teacher hadn't graded it yet.

*T*ara definitely has more activities than she can keep up with. Keeping in mind what you've learned about priorities, what advice would you give her?

_____

_____

Like Tara, maybe you feel you have too much going on in your life. Do you feel that you are running from lessons to clubs to teams to activities? All of your activities may be good ones, but are you finding it difficult to keep up with everything? If so, here is what should you do:

1. **Pray.** Ask God to help you decide which activities are best for you.

2. **Talk to your parents.** Discuss which things they feel are most important for you to do.

3. **Take the Apostle Paul's advice.**

Apostle Advice #1: You might think you can do anything, but not everything is good for you. Christians shouldn't allow any activity to take over their lives (see 1 Corinthians 6:12).

Your activities should be helpful to you in physical, mental or spiritual ways. Which of your activities are helpful to you?

_____

_____

Yet some of your activities might control too much of your time, thoughts, money or energy. If you have some of these types of activities, what can you do to keep them from taking over your life?

_____

_____

Apostle Advice #2: Honor

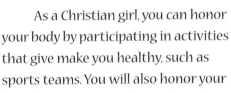

God with your body and do not harm it, for your body belongs to God (see 1 Corinthians 6:19-20).

As a Christian girl, you can honor your body by participating in activities that give make you healthy, such as sports teams. You will also honor your

Tiny Tip! Feeling pressured by all you have to do? Talk to your parents about planning a family fun day at the park.

body by staying away from drugs, tobacco and alcohol.

Name some activities you like to do that encourage you to honor your body.

_____

_____

Apostle Advice #3: In everything you do, glorify God

(see 1 Corinthians 10:31).

One of your desires should be to please God. Do your activities make God happy? If Jesus walked in during your club meeting or lesson, would you be glad to see Him or would you be embarrassed?

How can you glorify God in your activities?

_____

_____

Apostle Advice #4: Do your best at everything as if you are working for God (see Colossians 3:23).

Whether you are studying for a test, working on a gymnastics routine or memorizing a piano solo, you should give it your very best. Sometimes when people are involved in too many activities or in activities that they don't really care about, they find it hard to give their best. God wants you to do your best.

Are you able to give your best in all of your activities? Why or why not?

_____

_____

WRAPPING IT UP

Setting priorities means making decisions about what is most important. God and your family should be the most important things in your life. Other activities can be low or high priorities depending on your purpose statement. Read your purpose statement often to keep your priorities in order.

 ## Memory Verse

Before going on to the next chapter, write the memory verse for this chapter below. Memorize it!

_____

_____

Jot It Down

How can you decide which activities are best for you?

_____

_____

What changes would you like to make in your activities
or schedule?

_____

_____

Are You Puzzled? Set Priorities

You might need to figure out how to fit priorities in to
your schedule. Need some practice? Make these priorities fit into
the grid on the next page. Maybe some of these priorities are the
same as yours.

To do the puzzle, arrange the words to fit in the grid. Some
letters have been filled in to get you started. Hint: Begin with the
longer words. The solution is on page 207.

Word List

Band	Clubs	Prayer
Bible Reading	Family	School
Church	Friends	Sports
Choir	God	Youth Group
Chorus	Lessons	

Tip #5

Walk with God.

As the deer pants for streams of water, so my soul pants for you, O God.

~ Psalm 42:1

Kelsey opened her Bible and turned to the gospel of Mark for her daily reading. She read the passage and then answered the questions in her Bible study notebook. Kelsey had become interested in Bible reading and prayer at summer Bible camp. When she was there, everyone was on a "spiritual high," as the camp director called it. Reading the Bible and praying were exciting

there. God seemed to be really near, especially during the chapel session and the bonfire praise time.

When Kelsey returned home from camp, some of the excitement wore off, but she still continued to be faithful to daily

Bible reading and prayer. She tried to spend at least 10 minutes reading the Bible and five minutes praying every day. At first she did her "quiet time" in the morning, but then she realized she wasn't getting as much out of it as she should because she wasn't a morning person and she was still half-asleep. So she decided to read the Bible and pray right before bed instead. That way God's Word would be on her mind as she fell asleep. Still, even though Kelsey feels she is growing in her Christian life, she wonders if there is more she should be doing.

Growing as a Christian is an important part of your life. It is easy to get so caught up in other activities that Bible reading and prayer get neglected. In Chapter 5 you made a chart that included time to spend with God each day. Now that you've set aside that time, you need to use it. There are five things you can do to strengthen your spiritual life: keep a spiritual journal, read your Bible, pray, attend church and share your faith. Read on to find out more about these five faith-builders.

KEEPING A SPIRITUAL JOURNAL

Amber flipped her journal open to the prayer request section. Her friend Emily had asked for prayer for her grandmother. Amber wanted to write down Emily's prayer request so she wouldn't forget it. Since starting a spiritual journal three months before, Amber had found herself becoming more consistent in her Bible reading and prayer life, and she even listened better in church so that she could write down the things she learned from the pastor's message.

You may already have a journal or a diary in which you write about daily events and feelings so you can go back and read about them later. You can do the same with a spiritual journal. Your spiritual journal might be a three-ring binder or a spiral notebook – anything with paper. Label different sections of your spiritual journal for daily Bible reading, prayer requests, sermon notes and any others you want. Here are some ideas for what to write:

The Scripture reference from each day's Bible reading. Jot what you learn from the passage.

A prayer list. Write each request, the date you start praying for it, the date it is answered and how it is answered.

What you learn in **Sunday school** and during the **worship** service.

Ideas for serving God and others.

You can also glue or tape **Christian articles, poems or stories** you like in your journal.

Do you think keeping a spiritual journal would be helpful to you? Why or why not?

_____

_____

READING YOUR BIBLE

Alexa opened her Bible and began reading. She wanted to read through the Bible in a year (*After all, that's what really spiritual people do*, she thought). Reading Genesis hadn't been so bad because it had a lot of interesting stories in it. Then she read Exodus, which was mostly about Moses and the Israelites. That was interesting because she'd seen a movie about Moses.

But now Alexa was in the book of Numbers. She didn't understand the purpose of it! All of the "thou shalts" and "thees" and "thous" were hard to read, and she couldn't find anything that applied to her life.

Alexa didn't feel super spiritual reading through the Bible anymore. She felt bored!

Have you ever tried reading through the Bible? If so, what happened?

_____

_____

Just reading through the Bible doesn't make anyone extra spiritual. In fact, reading through the Bible can be difficult. The Old Testament has books that are filled with laws, facts and prophecies as well as those with familiar stories. The New Testament has some books, such as Revelation, that are hard to understand also.

However, wanting to read the Bible is great! Alexa should feel proud of herself that she has that desire, but she is making two mistakes. First, she needs to get a Bible translation that is easier for her to understand. There are many types of Bibles. Even though they all have the same message, they are written using different words. Like

Tiny Tip! Get a creation sensation: take your Bible outside and read it under a tree – or even in a tree!

Alexa, many people find the King James Version's "thees" and "thous" to be unfamiliar and hard to understand. Other Bibles, such as the New International Version, The Living Bible or the New International Reader's Version, are easier for kids to read.

Alexa's second mistake is she is reading Numbers, a book of the Bible that is difficult to understand. She enjoyed Genesis and Exodus because they had familiar stories. She might also enjoy the Old Testament book of Psalms, which are actually songs or poems, or Proverbs, which has an ideal 31 chapters for a month of reading. The book of Judges is full of exciting stories that you have probably heard in Sunday school. It tells about Gideon, Samson and the other men God used to defeat Israel's enemies. The book of Joshua talks about battles the Israelis fought.

The Gospels (Matthew, Mark, Luke and John) in the New Testament are also a good place to begin reading because they cover Jesus' life. Even though the Gospels tell many of the same stories, each book is a little different from the others.

What book of the Bible would you like to read?

Whichever parts of the Bible you choose to read, it's important that you are able to understand them. A good way to help your understanding is to make some notes in your spiritual journal.

First, write out the reference for what you are reading. To do that, write the name of the book, such as Genesis or Matthew. Then write the chapter number. After the number, put a colon (:). Then write the verses you read. Use a dash (-) between the first verse you read and the last. For example, the second chapter of Matthew, verses one through ten, would look like this: Matthew 2:1-10.

Second, for each reading write answers to the following:

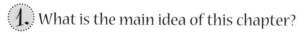
1. What is the main idea of this chapter?

2. Does God give me instructions?

3. Does God make me promises?

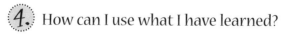
4. How can I use what I have learned?

You don't have to read straight through a book of the Bible, you can be like Elise and read different sections of the Bible to learn about certain things. Turn the page to see how she did it.

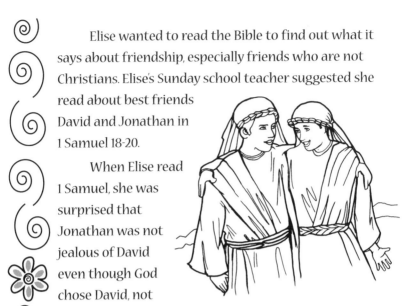

Elise wanted to read the Bible to find out what it says about friendship, especially friends who are not Christians. Elise's Sunday school teacher suggested she read about best friends David and Jonathan in 1 Samuel 18-20.

When Elise read 1 Samuel, she was surprised that Jonathan was not jealous of David even though God chose David, not Jonathan, to be king. Elise knew her friends were often jealous of each other about their gifts or clothes.

After reading 1 Samuel, Elise wondered what else the Bible said about friendship, but she wasn't sure how to find out. She did know she wasn't willing to read through the whole Bible looking for verses that mention friends!

Elise could benefit from a "concordance." A concordance is similar to a dictionary in that it has a lot of words listed in alphabetical order. After each word is a list of Bible verses that use that word. Some Bibles have a small concordance included in the back. You can also buy large concordances that have many words and references in them. Many web sites have free concordances, such as bible.gospelcom.net and bible.crosswalk.com.

Once she has a concordance, Elise could look up the words "friend" and "friendship" to find references for verses that discuss friends. If she did, she would find references such as Proverbs 17:17, Proverbs 18:24 and John 15:13-15. She might also want to look up other words that have to do with friendship such as "loyal" or "love."

There are all kinds of topics you can study in the Bible with the help of a concordance. "Love" is a good topic to study by itself. Or you might choose to study "anger," "patience," "peace," or "faith." Think of one topic (one word) you would like to study and write it here:

_____

Now look up your word in a concordance. Don't forget to also look up any words that are similar. Write the Bible references you find below.

_____

_____

Read a few verses from your list each day. Remember to write the reference and what you learn from each verse in your spiritual journal.

Do you plan to start reading your Bible if you haven't been? Don't give up! It takes time to get into the habit of reading your Bible each day. How will you get started?

_____

_____

 PRAYING

Dana listened as her Sunday school teacher talked about the importance of prayer. She felt guilty. She knew prayer was important, and many times she had resolved to pray every day. But she always gave up after a few days. Most of the time, Dana found her mind wandering in the middle of her prayer, or she couldn't think of anything to pray about.

Has that happened to you? Maybe you aren't sure how to get started or you have difficulty concentrating. There are lots of things you can do to work toward a better prayer life. Here are some ideas.

Keep a list. When a friend asks you to pray for her, write her name in your spiritual journal so you won't forget. Or say a silent prayer for her each time you see her.

Keep different lists of things to pray for each day. This is helpful if your list gets too long or if you get tired of praying for the same things every day. One day you might pray for certain friends, the next day pray for different friends and so on.

Use your fingers as a guide. Your thumb, which is closest to you, reminds you to pray for those closest to you: family and friends. The index finger is used to point. It reminds you to pray for those who point the way such as parents, teachers and pastors. Your middle finger, the strongest of all reminds you to pray for your leaders, such as the president. The fourth finger is your weakest. It reminds you to pray for those who are weak such as the sick and the homeless. The smallest finger reminds you to pray for yourself.

Write your requests on slips of paper and put them in a jar. Each time you pass the jar, take out a slip of paper and say a one-minute prayer for that request. Then put the slip of paper beside the jar. When the jar is empty, put all the slips back into it and start over, or add more.

Pray often for just a few seconds. As you get ready for school in the morning, say a quick prayer for your teachers. Pray for your dad or mom as you hear your parents leave for work. As

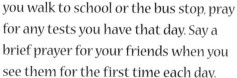

Walk with God.

you walk to school or the bus stop, pray for any tests you have that day. Say a brief prayer for your friends when you see them for the first time each day.

TiNY Tip! Prayer isn't just asking for things. Get a gratitude attitude by going outside and reflecting on the beauty of God's world. Then thank Him for all He made.

*T*here is no one place that is better for praying than others. Bible-time people prayed in lots of different places. For fun, draw a line between each person's name and the place he or she prayed.

___ 1. **Moses** (Exodus 1:9-10)　　**a. In battle with the Amorites**

___ 2. **Hannah** (1 Samuel 1:9-10)　**b. On Mount Sinai**

___ 3. **Jesus** (Matthew 26:36)　　**c. In a fish**

___ 4. **Paul and Silas** (Acts 16:23-25) **d. In the temple**

___ 5. **Jonah** (Jonah 2:1)　　　　**e. In jail**

___ 6. **Elijah** (1 Kings 18:20, 36-37)　**f. By a window**

___ 7. **Daniel** (Daniel 6:10)　　　**g. On Mount Carmel**

___ 8. **Joshua** (Joshua 10:12-13)　**h. In the Garden of Gethsemane**

Answers: 1-b, 2-d, 3-h, 4-e, 5-c, 6-g, 7-f, 8-a

These aren't the only places they prayed. We know Daniel also prayed in the lions' den as a witness to his belief in God's power to save him. Paul prayed everywhere he went on his mission trips. Jesus also prayed in a boat, in the mountain and in the desert. Wherever you pray, God can hear you.

Attending Church

Jana loved to go to Sunday school. She had lots of friends in her class. Some of them didn't go to her public school, so Sunday was the only time she saw them.

Jana really liked her teacher, Mrs. Carlson, too. Mrs. Carlson made the Bible lesson interesting by using stories, pictures and crafts. The problem was that Jana didn't enjoy the morning worship service. There were too many hymns, prayers and long sermons that were hard to understand. Jana found it hard to sit still so long and listen.

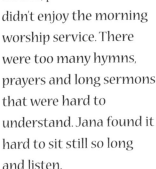

Do you ever feel like Jana? Lots of kids do. As you get older, you will understand the sermon more, but you can still get something out of the worship service now. Here are some ideas.

Choose your seat wisely. Your parents might insist that you sit with them during church. If not, ask a friend to sit with you. If you are allowed to sit with a group of friends, be sure they are friends who will pay attention during the service.

Take part in the singing. Some kids think it's not cool to sing, but God loves to hear you praise Him with music – even if your voice isn't CD quality! Think about the words you are singing. What messages do they offer? When a choir or individual sings, listen carefully to the words.

Follow the Scripture reading in your own Bible. If your pastor uses a more difficult translation, the words might be easier to understand in your Bible.

Try to learn three things from the sermon. You might not understand everything, but if you leave having learned three new things, you've done very well. Taking notes may help you follow the sermon. Try making a page in your spiritual journal that looks like this:

Date: _____

Scripture passage: _____

Title of sermon: _____

Main points:

1.

2.

3.

New things I learned:

1.

2.

3.

Ways to apply these things to my own life:

1.

2.

3.

SHARING YOUR FAITH

An important part of being a growing Christian is sharing your faith. You don't have to be a pastor, evangelist or missionary to share your faith. You can do it right in your classroom! Here are some ways that Christian girls have shared their faith.

Melissa D. of Elkins, West Virginia, was assigned to read a biography and give an oral report about it. She chose to read about Mary Slessor, a missionary who took the Gospel to Africa. Melissa told her public school class about Mary finding abandoned African babies and raising them herself. Melissa was able to share her own faith through her presentation about Mary Slessor.

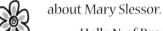

Holly N. of Brooklyn, New York, had to write a science report. She wrote about dinosaurs and the Bible. She explained that the Bible's book of Job talks about some big creatures that scientists believe might have been dinosaurs. Holly told how the earth's environment changed after the flood – there was colder weather and not as much food. She explained that this could have caused dinosaurs to become extinct.

Kristina G. didn't have any Christian friends at her school in Houston, Texas, so she asked Natasha, a non-Christian friend, to a youth pizza party at her church. Natasha kept coming to church with Kristina and eventually she became a Christian, too! Now she and Kristina are best friends. They are inviting more classmates to church.

Which of these ways to share your faith would be easiest for you?

_____

In what other ways could you share your faith at school?

_____

_____

WRAPPING IT UP

God promises that when you put Him first, you will have success. That may not mean you will be rich or famous. It does mean that you will have His peace and joy, and that your life will be full and satisfying. You will be your best.

Memory Verse

Before you go on to the next chapter, write the memory verse below. Memorize it!

_____

_____

Jot It Down

What things do you do every day that help you grow in your Christian life?

_____

_____

What new things can you do?

_____

_____

Prayer Jar

One of the prayer tips in this chapter was to write your prayer requests on slips of paper and put them in a jar. Make this colorful jar to promote prayer and pep up your room at the same time.

What You Need

* glass jar, any size
* several colors of tissue paper
* glue
* paint brush
* scissors

What to Do

1. Cut the tissue paper into small squares.

2. Paint a section of the jar with glue.

3. Stick the tissue squares on the glue.

4. Overlap the squares, adding more glue as needed.

5. Repeat until the whole jar is covered with paper. Do a second layer if you want.

6. Paint a thin layer of glue over the whole jar.

7. Allow the jar to dry overnight.

8. Fill the jar with your prayer slips. Each time you pass the jar, take out a slip and say a short prayer for that request. Place the slip of paper next the jar. When the jar is empty, put all of the slips back into it and start over or add more.

Cherish your family.

A<small>bove all, love each other deeply, because</small> love covers over a multitude of sins.

~ 1 Peter 4:8

E<small>lisabeth</small> sat in her room, pouting. She wanted to go to the mall with her friend Mindy and Mindy's mother. Mindy was going to shop for new clothes with her birthday money. Elisabeth didn't have any money to spend, but she knew it would be fun to

go along anyway – especially because Mindy's mom always bought them ice cream when they went to the mall!

But Elisabeth's mom wouldn't give her permission to go to the mall this time. Instead, her mom wanted Elisabeth to stay home for "family night." After attending a family life seminar at their church the weekend before, Elisabeth's parents had announced that Friday nights would be family nights. Each Friday, they said, one family member would choose something they would all do together.

"Time to start. Come and join us," Elisabeth's dad called upstairs to her.

Elisabeth dragged herself off her bed and reluctantly joined her two younger brothers, Steven and Micah, downstairs. Steven had gotten to choose what to do for the first family night because he was the youngest. He had decided they would rent a movie and eat pizza.

Elisabeth flopped onto a large pillow that was on the floor in front of the television. "What are we watching?" she asked.

"I couldn't make up my mind, so I got that new movie you've been wanting to see," Steven said.

"You chose one for me?" Elisabeth said.

"Yeah," Steven replied before cramming a piece of pepperoni pizza into his mouth.

Elisabeth sighed. Steven could be nice (even if he had the worst manners she'd ever seen!). Elisabeth helped herself to two

pieces of pizza and a can of soda, then settled in to watch the movie.

Elisabeth glanced around the room. Her mother was sitting in a rocking chair working on a cross-stitch project. Her dad was lying on the couch with Micah snuggled in next to him. Steven was sitting right in front of the television, still cramming pizza into his face.

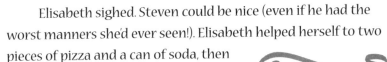

Do a random act of family kindness: Leave a secret note or gift for someone in your family.

This really isn't so bad, she thought. Steven and Micah are kind of cute, and Dad and Mom need a break from running us all over the place.

When the movie ended, Elisabeth said, "I'll get Steven and Micah into their pajamas and put them to bed."

"Yeah, and next week it's my turn to chose what to do!" Micah said.

Does your family have a special time to do things together? Being with your family is important. Friends come and go, but your family is forever. They are the ones who will always be there for you.

REAL Girls

WHAT IS A FAMILY?

Families are not all the same. Here are some different kinds of families in which girls your age live.

Stella A. lives with her mom and dad and two younger brothers in Manchester, New Hampshire.

Ling M., who was adopted from Vietnam, lives with her adoptive dad, mom and sister in La Cañada, California.

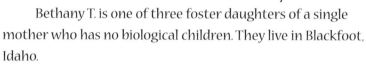

Ling

Autumn F. lives with her grandmother in Poughkeepsie, New York.

Bethany T. is one of three foster daughters of a single mother who has no biological children. They live in Blackfoot, Idaho.

Haley Y. is an only child who lives with her mother and father in Cumberland, Kentucky.

Rebekah L. lives with her mother and her sister, stepdad and three stepbrothers in Chicago, Illinois.

Sandra C. and her mother live with her grandmother in Jacksonville, Florida.

Rebekah

Jessica V. lives with her two parents and four older siblings in Columbus, Georgia.

Jewell G.'s mom died, so she now lives with just her dad and sister in Laurel, Delaware.

Which of these are "real" families? All of them! Families may have combinations of people who are related biologically, by marriage, by adoption or by foster care placement. No one type of family is the best. The important thing is to accept whatever type of family you have, and make the most of it.

What kind of family do you have?

_____

_____

Do all of your friends have the same kind of family as you? Tell about some of your friends who have different families.

_____

_____

_____

REAL Girls TOGETHER TIMES

Spending time together as a family creates strong bonds. You may have family projects you do together, a ministry you are involved in as a family, family vacation times or a weekly family night. All of these are ways to grow closer together as a family. Here are some things that girls your age do with their families.

Samantha V. and her family go camping together every summer. They cook over a campfire, hike and fish. At night they roast marshmallows and play card games or talk. They have fun even when it rains!

Rachel F.'s parents want their family to be together at home after church on Sundays in Mesa, Arizona, so they have fun as a family playing board games and popping popcorn.

Linzi T., who's from China, celebrates the Chinese New Year with her adoptive family every year. They make it as authentic as possible by dressing in traditional clothes and serving traditional foods. They also attend two ethnic festivals each year near where they live in Hot Springs, Arkansas. It's a lot of fun for all of them.

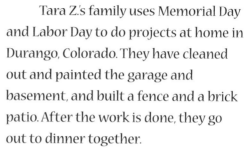

Tiny Tip! Get creative in a culinary way. See who in your family can build the largest ice cream sundae or create the pizza with the most unusual toppings (you only win if you eat what you make!).

Tara Z.'s family uses Memorial Day and Labor Day to do projects at home in Durango, Colorado. They have cleaned out and painted the garage and basement, and built a fence and a brick patio. After the work is done, they go out to dinner together.

Grace G.'s family volunteers at a pregnancy crisis center in Dayton, Ohio. They sort donated infant and maternity clothes, formula, diapers and car seats. They also help clean and repair the building.

LaKresha J. and her whole family swim on a swim team in Cleveland, Ohio. Her parents compete in the master's division. LaKresha and her two brothers compete in youth divisions. They try to see who can win the most events, but they also cheer for each other.

If your family isn't used to doing things together, maybe you can encourage them by suggesting activities to share. Here are a few ideas.

Games. Play a variety of board games based on skill or just for laughs. Not up for games? Try putting together a 500-piece (or larger!) puzzle.

Fitness. Find an activity that everyone in your family likes, such as walking, biking, in-line skating, swimming or hiking. You will improve your fitness level and tighten your family bond (and buns!) at the same time.

Projects. Suggest to your parents that the whole family tackle a big job together. Look around your house for ideas. Maybe you could put in a garden, build a fence, paint the garage, clean and organize the garage or basement or improve the lawn.

Ministry. Find a way to serve God and others as a family. Collect canned goods for a food bank or clothing for a homeless shelter, serve in a soup kitchen, paint a crisis pregnancy center or take part in a summer missions project.

What projects or activities do you do as a family?

_____

_____

What new things would you like to do together?

_____

_____

PARENTS ARE PEOPLE, TOO!

Do you ever wonder why your parents do the things they do? Do you wonder why they get angry when they find out you didn't do your homework or you haven't sorted the laundry like you said you would? Do you wonder why they limit the amount of time you spend watching television or using the computer?

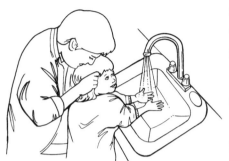

It's part of their "job" as parents, that's why!

Your parents were your first teachers. Your "lessons" began early in your life when your parents helped you to walk, wash your hands and use a spoon. The job didn't end then and it won't end for several more years. You don't need your parents to teach you the basics anymore, but they still will teach you about being responsible and making decisions.

What are some things your parents are teaching you right now?

_____

_____

Another job parents have is making sure you stay safe and healthy. That's why they might seem to worry too much about you. They can't help it! God gave them a built-in concern that makes them want to keep you safe. Sometimes their concern makes them react negatively — nag, get angry or yell — when you aren't home when you should be or when they find out you went somewhere they don't want you to be.

In what ways do your parents keep you safe and protected?

_____

_____

Parents also guide you. When you were little you told them everything — all about the worm you saw on the sidewalk, the doll your best friend got for her birthday and everything you did at school. Now you probably talk more to your friends than your parents. But it's difficult for your parents to get used to your not sharing with them as you once did. You might think your parents couldn't possibly understand, but maybe they can! They probably had friends who got mad and wouldn't talk to them, too. Just like you, they sometimes had problems with their teachers. Try talking to your parents the next time you have a problem.

In what ways can your parents guide you?

_____

_____

LiFE QUIZ! GETTING ALONG WiTH THE 'RENTS

How well do you get along with your 'rents (a much more fun way to say "parents"!)? Take this quiz and find out.

1. You are having a discussion with your dad about your report card. He says, "It looks like you aren't really trying." You say:

   a. "You always take the teacher's side!"

   b. "Can we sit down and talk about this?"

   c. "Who cares? I hate school!"

2. Your dad informs you that until you bring your math grade up to a "B" you won't be allowed to watch television or use the phone. You:

   a. Scream "That's not fair" and run out of the room.

   b. Pout and sulk around the house hoping he'll change his mind.

c. Determine to work hard to bring up your math grade.

3. Your mother notices that you are wearing eye shadow. She says, "Wash that stuff off your eyes before you leave this house!" You say:

　a. "You treat me like a baby!"

　b. "I never get to do anything!"

　c. "I'll wash it off but can we talk about this after school?"

4. You sit down to talk with your mother about the eye shadow. She explains that she doesn't want you to grow up too fast. She says you'll be allowed to wear eye shadow next year. You:

　a. Stomp out of the room.

　b. Plan to wear the eye shadow behind her back.

　c. Agree to wait or to talk about it again in a few months.

5. Your mother notices that you seem to be in a bad mood. She asks you what's wrong. You say:

　a. "Nothing" and then spend an hour on the phone telling your best friend all about what's bothering you.

　b. "Problems at school. Maybe you can help."

　c. "You'd never understand."

You could probably pick out the best answer easily, but is that how you really react to these and similar circumstances?

As you enter your teens, you may have more conflicts with your parents because you are becoming more independent. Gradually, you will be able to do more for yourself and you will want more freedom. This is normal, but it's important to keep a good relationship with your parents. Here are some suggestions.

Tiny Tip! It's OK to run away! When you are angry with your parents, run around the block twice or shoot 20 baskets to cool down before talking with them.

Keep talking to your parents.
Their advice comes from years of experience. They want to know what is going on in your life and they want to help you when you need it.

Pick a good time to talk about disagreements.
Don't try to talk to your parents when they first get home from work, or are hungry or tired. Wait until they're rested and in a good mood.

Be mature.
Whining, crying and yelling won't prove to them that you are growing up and capable of more freedom. Acting maturely will.

Be willing to compromise.
Sometimes everyone has to give a little to get what he or she wants. Try to think of alternate solutions that work for everyone.

Pray about your relationship with your parents.
God is interested in your family's joys and problems.

GETTING ALONG WITH SIBS

Lucy was in the living room working on her report about Mexico. She had carefully drawn an outline of Mexico and labeled the major cities. She sketched a picture of the country's flag and made a chart of Spanish words and what they mean in English. She'd written a one-page report in her neatest handwriting. Lucy had even included a picture of the Mexican boy her family sponsored through a Christian organization. Lucy was carefully fastening all the items to a large piece of poster board when her brother Brandon came into the room.

"What are you doing?" he said, stuffing a cookie into his mouth.

"Working on my project," she said.

Lucy looked up and saw Brandon drinking cherry punch. "You know you're not allowed to have drinks in here," she reminded him. "Take it to the kitchen."

"Okay, but I want to see your pictures first," Brandon said. As he leaned over her project to see the pictures, punch splashed out of his cup.

"Look what you did!" Lucy screamed. "You ruined my map and my report!"

"I'm sorry," Brandon said. "I didn't mean to do it."

"I can't believe you did that," Lucy said angrily. She stood up…

Write an ending for this story so that it turns out in a good way.

_____

_____

_____

_____

_____

Was it difficult to come up with a good ending? Making bad situations work out well can be hard to do in real life, too. Sibling relationships take a lot of work — but they can be lots of fun, too.

Sometimes your sibling might get on your nerves. And you might get on his or hers, too. But you and your siblings can also be good friends. Psalm 133:1 says, "How good and pleasant it is when brothers live together in unity!" Here are some ways to be friends with your sibs.

Spend **time** together — not just cleaning your room and doing dishes, but doing fun things, too. Play games, ride bikes or shoot baskets together.

Look for **common interests**. Find out what you both like to do. Are you both athletic? Try a new game together. Are you artistic? Make Christmas presents for your parents.

Be interested in your sibs. Ask about the things that are important to your sibling. Find out about his Cub Scout activities or her cheerleading tryouts.

Help each other. Work together on jobs and help each other in weak areas. Cleaning a room and doing homework are a lot more fun when you do it together.

Talk about problems. Don't let her messy side of the room start a war.

Talk about disagreements. Try to reach a compromise.

Work hard at sibling relationships. Siblings are friends for life!

REAL Girls

A Sad Note

Sometimes girls are abused by parents or older siblings. Abused girls are often embarrassed and don't want to talk to anyone about the abuse, but if you are being abused, remember that it is not your fault.

For example, Jamie R. was afraid to tell her mom the bad things her older brother made her do because Jamie was afraid her brother would say she was lying. Her brother was an honors student and a "model" son, while Jamie was often in trouble. Jamie was afraid her mother would believe her older brother and not her. In fact, when Jamie told her mother, she found out her mom had been suspecting the abuse. Together, the family got counseling. Jamie is now a happy high school junior.

Girls who are abused by parents are afraid to tell what is happening to them because they fear their parents might be put in jail and they would have to live in a foster home. This does happen sometimes. But everyone deserves a home where they feel safe and loved.

If there is abuse going on in your life, talk to a parent, teacher, counselor or pastor.

WRAPPING IT UP

Families are important. They are God's idea. He put people together in families to learn from each other, help each other and grow together. Make spending time with your family a priority.

Memory Verse

Before you go on to the next chapter, write the memory verse here. Memorize it!

_____

_____

Jot It Down

How can you improve your relationship with your mom and dad?

_____

_____

_____

How can you improve your relationships with your siblings?

_____

_____

 Family Love Pillow

This is a craft to do together as a family. Ask your parents first, then have each person in your family find a favorite worn piece of clothing that he or she is ready to part with. You will cut the clothing into squares and make a special family pillow. The colorful squares will remind you of each unique person in your family.

What You Need

* ❋ old clothing
* ❋ scissors
* ❋ fiberfill (available at craft or fabric stores)
* ❋ needle and thread or sewing machine
* ❋ iron

What to Do

1. Cut each piece of clothing until you have 24 squares that are 4"x 4" in size.

2. Arrange the squares into two piles of 12.

3. Arrange each pile of twelve into three rows of four squares.

4. Sew one square to the next, leaving a ½" seam. Make sure to stitch so that the seam is on the back of the fabric, not the front (see illustration).

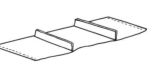

5. Keep sewing until you have three rows of four squares sewn together.

6. Ask an adult to iron the seams flat.

7. Sew the rows so that you have all twelve pieces sewn together.

8. Have an adult iron the seams flat again.

9. Go to your other 12 squares and repeat Steps 4-8.

10. Put the two sides of your pillow together with the fronts facing each other.

11. Sew around the edge, but leave a space large enough to fit in your hand.

12. Turn the pillow cover inside out so the good sides of the fabric are facing out.

13. Stuff with fiberfill.

14. Sew the hole closed.

Tip #7

Value your integrity.

The integrity of the upright guides them, but the unfaithful are destroyed by their duplicity.

~ Proverbs 11:3

 "Hey, Courtney, come here a minute," Dawn called out to her friend.

"What's up?" Courtney asked, joining the group of girls in the hall.

"Ashleigh saw the history test. She says there are four hard essay questions on it. She's going to tell us what they are so we can get our answers ready ahead of time."

"That's right," Ashleigh said. "I forgot my math homework

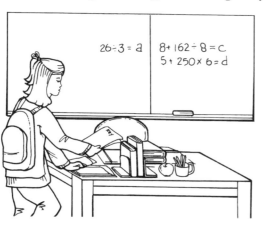

$26 \div 3 = a$

$8 + 162 \div 8 = c$
$5 + 250 \times 6 = d$

and when I went back into the room, tomorrow's history test was sitting right on top of Mrs. Miller's desk. I couldn't believe she just left it out in the open like that, so I figured if she was that dumb I could copy down

the four essay questions. Here, you guys can write them down from my paper."

The other girls began opening their notebooks to copy down the questions.

"Isn't that cheating?" Courtney asked.

"No, of course not," Ashleigh said. "We still have to study to get the answers ready. This will just help us all study better."

"But Mrs. Miller wants us to study everything, not just the answers to the questions," Courtney said.

"What's with you?" Dawn asked. "None of us did very well on the last history test. Now we have a chance to make up for it by getting a good grade. No one will know that we had the questions ahead of time."

"Yeah, but I'll know I had the questions ahead of time, and I know I'll feel guilty if I do this," Courtney said as she turned to walk away. "I guess you'll have to count me out."

TINY Tip! If you have to justify an action, it is probably the wrong thing to do.

Courtney faces a tough situation: whether or not to do something dishonest. If she had copied the essay questions, she would have been dishonest. Even though she might not have been caught cheating, Courtney would have known that she had cheated. She would have given up her integrity.

WHAT IS INTEGRITY?

When you have integrity, you are sticking to your morals and values. As a Christian, complete honesty should be part of your integrity — and that means choosing to be honest not just when other people know, but also when only you know. You can fool other people into thinking you are a girl of integrity, but you can't fool yourself, and you can't fool God. You and God know the truth. If you want to be your best, get in the habit of protecting your integrity by being totally honest.

DOING THE HONEST THING

It's not always easy to have integrity. Read on for some examples of girls who found it difficult to be completely honest.

Jenilee carefully finished her sketch. She had drawn a picture of her dog, Sunny, running on the beach. She put her name on the back and handed it to Mrs. Maxfield. Jenilee hoped her picture would win the contest. She looked around at the students who were still drawing. She couldn't tell what some of the drawings were supposed to be, but she saw that Kristin and Lydia were both working hard on good drawings. Kristin had sketched her cat sitting in the window, and Lydia had drawn a garden.

"Okay," Mrs. Maxfield said, "Our time is up. Please turn in your entries."

"I'm not quite done," Lydia said. "Can I finish mine at home and bring it back tomorrow?"

"No. The rules said that all drawings have to be completed in class," Mrs. Maxfield said. "Besides, the committee is going to judge the pictures this afternoon."

Jenilee wanted to stay and watch Mrs. Maxfield

hang the pictures on the bulletin board after school, but she had a science club meeting. After her meeting was over, Jenilee realized she had forgotten her social studies book. She ran back to her classroom to get it. As she left the classroom, Jenilee stopped to look at all of the pictures on the bulletin board.

Some of these are really good, Jenilee thought. I

don't have a chance of winning up against them.

As she glanced at each student's work, Jenilee realized that Kristin's cat picture wasn't on the bulletin board. She turned to look around the room, and then she spotted the edge of it sticking out from under Mrs. Maxfield's desk. She must have dropped it as she was hanging the ones on the bulletin board.

Jenilee found herself in a dilemma. Mrs. Maxfield was unlikely to find the picture under her desk, which meant the judges wouldn't see it and Jenilee's picture would have a better chance of winning. But at the same time, Jenilee would never know if her picture was really the best or not if one of the best entries was missing.

What should I do? Jenilee thought.

What would you do if you were Jenilee? Write the ending to the story.

_____

_____

_____

_____

_____

Bethany thoughtfully read the questions on her geography test. She had answered all but two, and she was sure the ones she'd answered were right.

"Name the two deserts in South America," Bethany read. She had studied for the test but couldn't think of these final answers.

Just then Candice raised her hand. "I'm done with my test," she said to Mrs. Alapo.

Mrs. Alapo walked toward Candice. As Candice handed her test to Mrs. Alapo, Bethany saw the answers

she was missing: the Atacama and Patagonia Deserts.

Oh, I remember now, Bethany thought, writing them down on the blank lines.

Bethany raised her hand, "I'm done, too."

Mrs. Alapo came to get Bethany's test. Bethany pulled out her book for free reading and opened to the marked place. Then she thought about the test.

Would I have remembered the answer without seeing Candice's answer? she wondered. *Was it fair to write down the answers after I saw them?*

Bethany wondered what she should do. She hadn't meant to cheat, but she wanted a perfect score. She had studied hard to get it.

What would you do if you were Bethany?

_____

_____

_____

_____

Did you finish the first story by having Jenilee tell Mrs. Maxfield about Kristin's picture or having Jenilee fasten the picture to the bulletin board? It would be difficult for Jenilee to do either of those things. It might mean she would come in second place to Kristin's picture, or maybe she would come in first. Maybe neither of those pictures would win. If Jenilee chose to leave Kristin's picture under Mrs. Maxfield's desk, no one but her would know. But Jenilee would know, and God would know, and that's what's really important.

In the second story, did you have Bethany tell Mrs. Alapo that she'd seen Candice's paper? That would be really hard to do, too. Bethany wouldn't know ahead of time if Mrs. Alapo would accept the answers, give her a new question or count them wrong and say Bethany had cheated. Again, only Bethany and God would ever know. But that's what integrity is all about: being completely honest even if no one else knows.

A DISHONEST DUO

If being honest is often difficult for you, don't think you're alone. God knew we would need advice on how to be honest, so He gives many examples of dishonesty and its results in the Bible.

One story is about a married couple named Ananias and Sapphira, who owned some land (see Acts 5:1-10). One day they decided to sell the land. When they did, the money was theirs to spend however they liked. Ananias and Sapphira decided to give some of the money to the church. That was a good, honest thing to do! But Ananias, with Sapphira's blessing, told everyone that this offering was all of the money they received for the land, rather than just some of it. Ananias and Sapphira ruined their integrity.

God informed Peter that Ananias was lying. When Peter asked Ananias about it, Ananias lied.

So Peter said to him, "Ananias, why did you let Satan rule your heart? You lied to the Holy Spirit. You lied to God, not to men!"

Then Ananias fell down dead! Three hours later Sapphira came to see Peter. Not knowing what had happened to her husband, she too lied and then fell down dead!

Try the quiz below and see if you can match other Bible people to the lies they told. Two different people told the lie "she is my sister," so you will need to use it twice.

1. Satan (Genesis 3:4)

A. She is my sister.

2. Potiphar's wife (Gen. 39:17)

B. They were here but they've left.

3. Ananias (Acts 5:1)

C. You can have her if you work seven years for her.

4. Jacob (Genesis 27:19)

D. You will not die.

5. Saul (1 Samuel 18:17)

E. I did not laugh.

6. Rahab (Joshua 2:5)

F. I didn't keep part of the money for myself.

7. Abraham (Genesis 12:13)

G. If you fight in battle I will give you my older daughter.

8. Sarah (Genesis 18:15)

H. He made sport of [attacked] me.

9. Isaac (Genesis 26:7)

I. I am your firstborn.

10. Laban (Genesis 29:19)

Answers: 1. D, 2. H, 3. F, 4. I, 5. G, 6. B, 7. A, 8. E, 9. A, 10. C

DISHONESTY HAS CONSEQUENCES

Lying, misleading, cheating and stealing are all ways of being dishonest. Each time you do these things, you face consequences. Sometimes it means being punished by parents and teachers. Or it may mean parents, teachers or friends lose their trust in you. Other times, when no one but you and God know what you did, it means a loss of your sense of integrity. Here are some situations where girls weren't honest and faced the consequences.

Amanda felt left out because her friends had friendship bracelets and she didn't. Many stores sold the bracelets, but they were $4.99. That was $4.99 more than Amanda had!

So to get a bracelet, Amanda decided that she would shoplift, just this once. But as Amanda pocketed the bracelet, a sales clerk saw what she did. The clerk stopped Amanda as she was leaving the store, and the store manager called Amanda's mom. He told them Amanda wasn't allowed to shop in that store anymore. Later at home, Amanda's mom punished her by saying she could not go shopping alone or with friends anymore.

What could Amanda have done to get the bracelet without shoplifting?

_____

_____

How can Amanda regain her mom's trust and her own sense of integrity?

_____

_____

Alicia was home by herself and getting dressed for school. She was supposed to finish getting ready to leave for school by 7:45. Her mom had left for work and her older sister had just left for school. Alicia would be late if she didn't hurry!

Alicia couldn't find a shirt she wanted to wear, so she borrowed her older sister's favorite shirt. She figured she'd tell Dana about it that evening.

But at lunch, Alicia spilled chocolate milk on the shirt. She knew Dana would be mad at her! She ran all the way home after school and hid the shirt under her bed, hoping to wash it later when no one else was around to see her.

When Dana got home from school, she told Alicia she was going to go to the mall with her friends. She wanted to change into her favorite shirt.

"Have you seen my shirt?" Dana asked Alicia. "I was sure I put it in my drawer."

"No. I don't know where it is," Alicia said. "Maybe it's still in the dirty clothes pile."

"I don't have time to look now," Dana said. "Jennifer is waiting for me."

After Dana left, Alicia's friend called. By the time she was off the phone, Alicia had forgotten all about the shirt. That night, Alicia and Dana were watching TV when they heard their mom, who was vacuuming, call from upstairs.

"Alicia," her mom yelled from upstairs, "why is Dana's dirty shirt wadded up under your bed?"

Dana turned to Alicia, "You knew where my shirt was! You took it and then hid it!"

Alicia's mom was able to get the shirt clean, but Dana wouldn't let Alicia borrow her clothes anymore, even if she did ask first.

What should Alicia have done differently?

_____

_____

How can she get Dana to forgive her?

_____

_____

Shannon always got a 100 percent on her spelling test. One week she didn't have as much time to study, and she was afraid she would flunk the test. So she decided to make a "cheat sheet" just in case she forgot how to spell one of the words. She left it on the edge of her desk.

But as Mrs. McKenzie said the spelling words, Shannon realized she knew all of them without looking

at her cheat sheet. She even forgot it was there.

As Mrs. McKenzie walked around the

room repeating the words, she saw Shannon's cheat sheet.

"I didn't use it," Shannon said.

"I'm really surprised at you, Shannon," Mrs. McKenzie said. "I don't know whether you used it or not so I am going to have to give you a zero. You need to have your parents sign your test tonight so I know you talked with them about this."

Shannon tried to explain to her parents why she'd had the cheat sheet, but they were disappointed in her.

"It doesn't matter whether you cheated or not," her dad said. "You were planning to cheat if you needed to do it."

Shannon knew it would be a long time before her parents or teacher trusted her again. She wished she'd never thought about cheating.

What should Shannon have done instead of cheating?

_____

_____

What can she do now to fix the situation?

_____

_____

How to Be Totally Honest

Learning to be totally honest isn't always easy. But when you're a person of integrity, you can be proud of yourself and know that God is proud of you, too.

How can you learn to be totally honest? Here are a few ideas:

Ask God to help you. Since honesty is His idea, He'll be glad to support you!

Figure out why you are tempted to lie, cheat, mislead or steal. Are you trying to hide something wrong you've done? Are you trying to impress someone? Are you afraid of failing? Are you trying to be part of the in-crowd? Think about your reason, then ask God to help you find another answer than dishonesty.

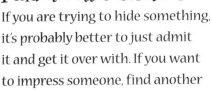

Tiny Tip! When you feel like you are alone in choosing the right action, remember that Jesus is with you.

Find a better solution.

If you are trying to hide something, it's probably better to just admit it and get it over with. If you want to impress someone, find another

way to impress him or her without making something up. Chances are that person will like you just as you are anyway. If you're afraid of failing, maybe a friend or teacher can help you develop some better study skills.

Talk to an adult. Your parents, Sunday school teacher or pastor want to work with you to be a person of integrity. Ask one of them to help you find a solution.

How will you learn to be honest?

_____

_____

WRAPPING IT UP

Being a person of integrity is really important! Make it a habit to always be honest and you'll never get a reputation for being a liar or cheater. People (including you!) will be able to trust you. That's a really good feeling.

Memory Verse

Before you go on to the next chapter, write the key verse on the lines below.

_____

_____

Jot It Down

Think of a time when you weren't totally honest. What happened?

_____

_____

How did you feel afterward?

_____

_____

What could you have done differently?

_____

_____

 Dial-a-Message Puzzle

Being a Christian girl of integrity is important. What can you do when you're tempted? Solve the puzzle below to find a message from God that will help you know what to do.

Each blank below has a number below it. Read a number and find it on the phone on the next page. You have three choices for the correct letter but only one is right! Guess which letter to use in the puzzle. If you aren't sure, write all three, then cross off the wrong ones when you get more clues. Some of the letters have been filled in to help you get started.

___ ___ B ___ ___ T
 7 8   6 4

___ O ___ ___ S ___ L ___ E ___ ,
9   8 7   3 8   7

___ H ___ ___ , ___ O ___ ___ D.
8   3 6   8   4 6

___ E ___ ___ S ___ ___ H ___
7   7 4 8   8 3

Value Your Integrity.

___ ___ V ___ L, ___ ___ D H ___
 3   3   4   2   6   3

W ___ L ___ ___ L ___ ___
   4   5   3   3   3

___ ___ ___ M Y ___ ___.
 3   7   6   6   8

— James 4:7

Tip #8

Be compassionate.

And what does the Lord require of you? To act justly and to love mercy and to walk humbly with the Lord your God.

~ **Micah 6:8**

Heather entered her Sunday school classroom and sat down. Her teacher wasn't there yet, so all the girls were sitting around discussing their week at school. They were all talking at once when the door opened. It got quiet in the room as a new girl entered.

Heather looked at the new girl. She was wearing a dress that looked a size too small and like it had been washed too many times. It was so faded Heather wasn't sure what color the dress had originally been! The girl wore white bobby socks and black dress shoes. Her hair hung limply around her face. A couple of the other girls nudged each other and started whispering. The rest of the girls continued discussing school.

She looks lost, Heather thought. *And she must know she isn't dressed like the rest of us.*

Heather remembered how she'd felt coming to Sunday school for the first time just a few months before. She'd been dressed the same as the other girls, but she'd still felt a bit afraid and shy. She thought about how her teacher Mrs. Gray had made her feel so welcome.

I wish Mrs. Gray would hurry and get here, Heather thought.

She always knows the right thing to say and she makes everyone feel so welcome.

But Mrs. Gray was late, and Heather knew she had to do something. Fast.

Taking a deep breath, Heather quickly said to the new girl, "Come on in. My name's Heather. You can sit by me." Heather moved down one chair, leaving the chair on the end for the new girl.

The girl looked relieved as she sat in the chair next to Heather. Heather felt the rest of the girls staring at her. She didn't look back because she knew if she did, she'd see disapproval in their eyes.

Heather turned away from the other girls and faced the new girl. "It's kind of hard being the new girl, isn't it?" she asked.

When Heather realized how the new girl felt and did something about it, she was showing "compassion."

WHAT IS COMPASSION?

Compassion is when you feel you understand someone else's suffering and want to help. Heather understood how the new girl was "suffering" by being new and unsure of herself. Heather helped her by reaching out and welcoming her, even though she knew the other girls might not understand. Compassion is not always easy!

Jesus is our best example of someone who showed compassion to others.

A few of those instances are listed on the next page. As you read each one, write how Jesus showed compassion, then how you might face a similar situation.

Be Compassionate.

Jesus had compassion for the crowd of people because they were helpless, like sheep without a shepherd. (Matthew 9:36, Mark 6:34)

Jesus showed compassion by:

_____

If I were in this situation I could show compassion by:

_____

Jesus felt compassion toward the crowd and healed the sick. (Matthew 14:14)

Jesus showed compassion by:

_____

If I were in this situation I could show compassion by:

_____

Jesus felt compassion toward the crowd of 4,000. They had been with Him three days and had nothing to eat, so He performed a miracle and fed them with bread and fish. (Matthew 15:32, Mark 8:2)

Jesus showed compassion by:

_____

If I were in this situation I could show compassion by:

_____

ARE YOU COMPASSIONATE?

Take this quiz to see how compassionate you are.

1. A new student comes to school. She doesn't speak much English, only Spanish. She seems very sad. You:

    a. Smile at her.

    b. Do nothing. After all, you don't know Spanish!

    c. Try to communicate friendship without words by smiling and gesturing to her to sit by you at lunch.

2. You see in the newspaper that there are many families living in your town's homeless shelter. The pictures show girls your age there. You:

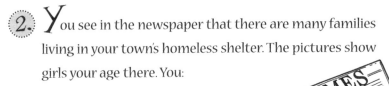

    a. Pray for them.

    b. Sort through your bulging closets and drawers for clothes to donate.

    c. Think, "I'm glad that's not me."

3. Your mom thinks it would be a good idea to sponsor a child in a poor country. She asks you if you would be willing to help. You:

    a. Offer to give up part of your allowance and recycle soda cans for extra money to give.

    b. Say that you'll help when you're older and can earn more money.

    c. Try to not ask for extras at the grocery store.

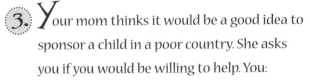

4. *T*anya is a special education student who joins your class for P.E. She is always the last chosen for a team. You can see the hurt in her eyes. Today it's your turn to be team captain for volleyball. You:

    a. Choose her after you get all the really good players on your team.

    b. Choose her first, then the really good players.

    c. Ignore her until she's the last one.

5. *Y*ou get home from school and plan to ask your mom if you can go to your friend's house until suppertime. When you go to ask, you find her in the kitchen. Your little brother is hanging on her leg while she's trying to cook. You notice that she looks tired and frustrated. You:

    a. Ask to go to your friend's house.

    b. Offer to take your little brother to the park so your mom can have some peace.

    c. Ask to go to your friend's house, but offer to do the dishes after supper.

Score yourself and see how you did!

1. a. 3 points. A good start, but you need to do more to welcome her.

    b. 0 points. You don't have to use words to show friendship!

    c. 5 points. Good for you! You are showing compassion.

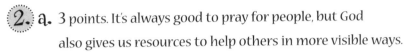
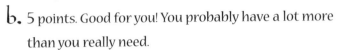

2. **a.** 3 points. It's always good to pray for people, but God also gives us resources to help others in more visible ways.

b. 5 points. Good for you! You probably have a lot more than you really need.

c. 0 points. What if it were you someday? What would you want others to do for you?

3. **a.** 5 points. Good for you! You realize that you can make a difference.

b. 0 points. Even small amounts of money help.

c. 3 points. That helps cut down on the grocery bill. How about kicking in a little of your own money? Why not ask for one less Christmas present and let that money be a gift for a child living in poverty?

4. **a.** 3 points. It's good that you want to choose her, but the other captain can't steal all the good players at once. You could chose her first and still get some top players.

b. 5 points. Good for you! You just made her day!

c. 0 points. How would you feel if you were chosen last every time?

5. **a.** 0 points. If you plan on enjoying the food, why not pitch in and help your tired mom?

b. 5 points. Good for you! You realized your mom needs a break more than you need to see your friend.

c. 3 points. The offer to help is good, but why not help now instead of later?

Total: _____

If you scored 20-25: You are a truly compassionate person, just as Jesus was.

If you scored 15-20: You have a good start on compassion.

If you scored below 15: You need to start thinking about how others feel and what you can do about it.

SHOWING COMPASSION

There are many simple ways to show compassion. Make a check next to those you have done or plan to do this week.

____ Encourage a student who gets a poor test grade.

____ Offer to help someone with his homework.

____ Sit with someone who is alone in the lunchroom, or invite her to sit with you.

____ Invite a new student to your house after school.

____ Tell someone "good try" when he tries and fails.

____ Help a student who has dropped her lunch tray.

____ Help a teacher clean the classroom after school.

____ Do the dishes when it's not your turn.

____ Baby-sit a sibling so your mom can have some free time.

____ Cook supper or help with it.

____ Encourage your mom and dad when they look tired.

____ Offer to get your mom and dad something to drink when they come home from work so they can relax.

____ Donate unused clothes, toys and books to a homeless shelter or other organization.

____ Buy cans of food for the food bank with your allowance.

What other ideas do you have for showing compassion this week?

_____

_____

Here are two unfinished stories. Read each story and write an ending that shows compassion.

Jasmine ran up the sidewalk to the school. She'd gotten up late and had to get dressed and eat breakfast in a hurry. Then when she went to get her bike to ride to school, she found that it had a flat tire, so she'd had to walk.

Jasmine hurried to her locker, opened it and grabbed her notebook and books. At the locker next to her, Josh was trying to get his stuff out of his locker. Most of the students thought Josh was a little strange and ignored him.

Josh gave a final tug on his books and they all tumbled to the floor. Papers spilled out of his notebook and his lunch hit the ground. An apple rolled a few feet down the hallway.

Jasmine glanced over at Josh. He looked like he wanted to cry. A few kids were still standing around the lockers. A few snickered; the rest gawked at him. Looking at the clock, Jasmine saw that the bell was about to ring.

Be Compassionate.

So Jasmine…

_____

_____

_____

_____

_____

*T*asha felt the hot sun on her back as she waited for her turn in the relay. She knew this event was really important. If her relay team won, their school would win the meet and be the city champions.

Tasha glanced back and saw her teammate approaching. She took the baton in a smooth move and sprinted as fast as she could. She prepared to pass it to Shawna, the last person on the relay team.

Shawna grabbed the baton from Tasha. As she started to sprint she dropped the baton, stepped on it and fell. Their relay team placed last. Instead of getting the championship, Tasha's school placed third.

Tasha watched as Shawna walked toward the bus, her head down. No one said anything to her. Instead, they gave her mean looks. Tasha knew Shawna must feel badly, but so did she. She had wanted to win the championship.

153

So Tasha…

_____

_____

_____

_____

_____

 ✻REAL✻ Girls

COMPASSION iN ACTioN

Here are some ways girls put compassion in action.

Lena S. of Appleton, Wisconsin, cleans out her closet and drawers every year. She donates the unused items to a charity. Last year her stuff went to Bosnia.

Jasmine L. of Bradenton, Florida, walks dogs to earn money for a child her family sponsors in Peru through a Christian organization.

Tiffany C. of Opelika, Alabama, is a greeter for her church's Sunday school. She helps welcome all of the new kids and shows them their classrooms.

Meaghan R. of Columbus, Ohio, is a peer tutor at school. She helps students with their homework. She helps them understand things that they don't understand during class.

Try one of these ideas, or come up with your own!

WRAPPING IT UP

Compassion is sympathy in action. It's knowing how someone feels and doing something about it. It may be as simple as smiling, introducing yourself, saying a kind word or giving some help. You can learn to be a compassionate person. Start today!

Memory Verse

Before going on to the next chapter, write the memory verse below. Memorize it!

_____

_____

Jot It Down

Think of a time when someone was compassionate to you. What did he or she do?

_____

_____

How did it make you feel?

_____

Do you consider yourself a compassionate person? Why or why not?

_____

_____

Heart Mobile

There are lots of ways to show compassion. This mobile will remind you of ways to be compassionate every day.

What You Need

- ❋ two straws
- ❋ yarn
- ❋ red construction paper
- ❋ scissors
- ❋ tape
- ❋ pen or marker

What to Do

1. Cut five hearts from construction paper.

2. On each heart, write one way that you can be compassionate every day. Some ideas: "Smile at someone who looks sad," "Talk to someone I don't know who needs a friend" and so on.

3. Tape the two straws together to form an X.

4. Tape a piece of yarn to each heart and tie each one to the straws.

5. Tie one piece of yarn to the top of the straws to hang the mobile in your room.

Be content.

I have learned to be content whatever the circumstances.

~ Philippians 4:11

Julia sat on her friend Morgan's bed. They were working on a social studies project together.

"I can't believe your parents let you have a TV in your bedroom," Julia said. "I'm not

even allowed to watch TV on school nights. I only get to watch two hours Friday night and two on Saturday. How'd you talk them into your own television?"

"I didn't. They gave it to me for my birthday. That way I can watch what I want in here and they can watch what they want in the family room," Morgan said.

"You have your own stereo, too!" Julia said, noticing the top-of-the-line system on Morgan's nightstand.

"That was my Christmas present," Morgan said. "They always buy me big presents — television, stereo, mountain bike, ski equipment and stuff like that. But the thing is, they're so busy working to make money to buy stuff that they never have time to do anything with me."

"That's too bad," Julia said. "I would like to have my own TV so I don't have to watch cartoons like my little brothers do, but if I had to choose I'm glad my parents have time to do things with me. Like this Sunday we're going hiking. I guess I've always taken it for granted."

Even though Julia wouldn't mind having more "things," she is content with what she has. She has something important that Morgan doesn't have: her parents' time and attention.

WHAT IS CONTENTMENT?

Contentment is being happy with what you have, whether you have a lot like Morgan or less like Julia. Being content also means being happy with yourself and with the circumstances you are in.

When people aren't content with what they have, they often make plans to get what they want. That might mean working long hours to buy something and saving money until they can get it. But sometimes wanting things too much can lead to bad situations, such as building up a lot of debt or even stealing. People who are not content may even waste their lives being bitter about the things they can't have.

Tiny Tip! Help others to be content. Bring an extra treat in your lunch to share with someone who doesn't have one.

Discontentment comes in other areas as well. People can be unhappy about income, education or employment, or about the way they look. They might be discontent with their abilities — maybe they want to be the smartest in the class or the fastest runner on the team.

This doesn't mean that it's wrong to want to improve yourself. Being your best is important. But when you want what you can't have, or you are unhappy with how God made you, your discontentment can cause you trouble. Learning to be content with what God has given you is important.

 **LiFE QUIZ!**

Are You Content?

Are you learning to be content? Take this quiz and find out.

1. Your friend invites you to celebrate her birthday with her family. When you get to her house, you can't believe the enormous pile of presents! She gets a CD player and CDs, clothes and a new bike. You, on the other hand, ride your brother's old 10-speed. You want a CD player but your dad says you have to save your allowance to pay for half of it. You:

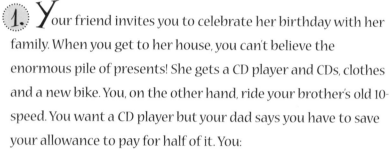

a. Wish your parents had as much money as her parents did.

b. Are glad your dad is willing to pay for half the CD player.

c. Plan to spend more time with your friend and use her things.

2. Your friend and her family are going on a two-week Disney World vacation this summer. You've always wanted to go there, but instead you know your family will spend a week at the lakeside cottage you go to every year. You:

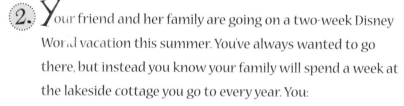

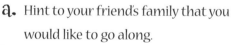

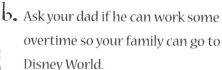

a. Hint to your friend's family that you would like to go along.

b. Ask your dad if he can work some overtime so your family can go to Disney World.

c. Are thankful that you get to have a week's vacation with your family, even if it is at the same lake every year.

3. Your best friend has thick, dark hair, dark eyes and creamy skin. You inherited your dad's red hair and freckles. You:

a. Are envious of your friend's looks.

b. Beg your parents to let you dye your hair.

c. Decide to like yourself and the unique looks you have.

4. You plan to ride your bike to school but you have a plain bike with no gears. You ask your dad if you can have a new bike. He says money is tight and you'll have to ride your old one until at least Christmas. You:

a. Remind him that all of your friends have 10-speed bikes.

b. Thank him for considering it and ride your old bike a while longer.

c. Walk to school so no one will know you don't have a 10-speed.

5. You are back-to-school clothes shopping with your mom. You want the same kind of jeans that all your friends have, but your mom insists on plain, no-brand jeans because you can get three pairs for what you would pay for one pair of the others. You:

a. Accept the no-name brand and ask your mom to help you improve them by adding appliques and beads.

b. Refuse to wear them.

c. Remind her how it feels to be left out.

:

Answers

1. b. It takes a lot of maturity to accept that your parents can't give you as much as your friend's parents give her. But when you think about it, who really needs that much stuff anyway?

2. c. Sometimes a less expensive, simpler vacation is more fun. You'll have lots of time to be with your family, talk, lay in the sun and swim. In the long run you will have as many happy memories as your friend. Maybe more!

3. c. Don't waste your life fretting about what you can't change. We live in a diverse nation. People come in all sorts of colors, shapes and sizes with multitudes of hair colors and styles. Decide to find the best hairstyle and look for you, and then be happy with it.

4. b. It's tough to not have what most of the other girls have! And it's hard to remind yourself that it's who you are and not what you have that's important. But that's what you have to do this time. Start looking for ways to earn some of the money yourself!

5. a. Make the best of the situation. Go to a craft or sewing store and look for ways to fix up your jeans to reflect your personality.

Did you choose all the right answers? You probably did, but it's much harder to make those choices in real life!

CONTENTMENT CRISIS

In the following story, Mikayla is having trouble being content with what she has. She feels left out and that she's being treated unfairly. (Maybe you have felt the same way!) Read the story and write an ending that solves the problem.

Mikayla is on the girls' basketball team. Most of the girls on the team have name-brand shoes for practices and games. Mikayla is still wearing her old, no-name shoes that her mom bought for her at a discount store.

"Mom," Mikayla pleaded. "Everyone else has cool shoes. I'm the only one left out. Why can't I get some?"

"I'm not paying $75 for shoes that you'll probably outgrow in six months. I'll get you new shoes, but I'm not paying over $25."

"But we won't be able to get any like that for $25!" Mikayla exclaimed.

"Maybe we can find some that look almost the same," her mom rationalized.

"But it won't be the same. The other girls will know the difference!"

"If you want $75 shoes, you will have to come up with the other $50 yourself," her mom said.

"How am I supposed to do that?" Mikayla asked.

"You'll think of something if you want them badly enough," her mom said. "Otherwise you'll have to be content with $25 shoes."

"It's not fair," Mikayla yelled, running from the room.

Try to write an ending that works for everyone.

_____

_____

_____

_____

Did you find a way for Mikayla and her mother to compromise or for Mikayla to be able to accept her mom's decision? Sometimes it's hard to come up with real-life solutions, especially when your friends have things that you don't have.

Discontentment doesn't always have to do with wanting things that can be purchased. Here is another contentment crisis about a girl who was unhappy with her situation.

Kate sat in the school auditorium waiting for her turn to try out for the spring musical. She was a little nervous, but not too much. She was used to singing solos because she did it at her church. She'd been singing in public for a couple of years now and had gotten over the jitters long ago. Now she felt confident and prepared.

Kate's name was called and she went up front. She handed Mr. Turner the music she had chosen. She began her piece right on cue and sang it without mistakes.

"I should get the lead," she told her friend Julie. "I was the best one there."

Early the next morning at school, Kate ran to the bulletin board outside the music room to see the cast list. She wasn't the lead. Not only that, she didn't even have a solo. She was just part of the chorus!

"I don't know why I didn't get the lead or even a solo!" she exclaimed to Julie. "I'm only in the chorus!"

"It looks like the eighth graders got all the solos," said Julie as she examined the list. "Maybe Mr. Turner gave them the solos because it's their last year at middle school. You still have two more years to be in the musicals. Maybe they just have more experience, too."

"I don't care," Kate said. "If I can't have a solo, I don't want to be in it."

"Why not?" asked Julie. "Being in the chorus will be fun. We can sit together! And you still get to perform. Besides, it will be a chance for you to get lots of experience so you'll have a better chance next year."

"I don't care," Kate said. "If I can't have a part, I'm not going to be in it!"

In what way was Kate not content?

_____

How would this story have been different if Kate had been content? Write a better ending here.

_____

_____

_____

_____

_____

Tell about a time you felt discontented like Mikayla or Kate. How did you handle it? Could you have reacted differently?

_____

_____

_____

Learning to Be Content

Learning to be content isn't always easy, but you will be happier if you are. Here are some ways to be content:

Make a list of all the good things in your life: family, friends, food, pets, talents, abilities or anything positive.

Take time to **thank God** each day for the things on your list.

Vow to **stop comparing** what you have with what others have.

Be happy when others get good things. The Bible says to rejoice with those who rejoice (see Romans 12:15).

Stay away from situations that cause you to be discontent, such as going to the mall when you know you don't have the money to buy anything.

Pray daily for others who have less than you do.

Tiny Tip! Show you're content: Write a thank-you note to a parent or teacher for something they have done for you.

Wrapping It Up

Being content means accepting the things that you own, the abilities and talents God has blessed you with, and the looks He has given you. It means not envying those who have more or coveting the things they have. When you can thank God for what He has given you, and decide that it is enough for you, then you are content.

Memory Verse

Before going on to the next chapter, write the memory verse here. Say it often, especially when you want something you can't have.

_____

_____

Jot It Down

Being thankful for what you have helps you to be content with what you have. Think of some things for which you are thankful. Make a list below.

_____

_____

_____

When is it most difficult for you to be content? What can you do about it?

_____

_____

_____

Thankfulness Calendar

Part of being content is to be thankful for what you have. If you spend a lot of time thinking about things that you wish you could have, you will find it hard to be content. This calendar will help you think about what you have rather than what you want!

What You Need

* colored poster board
* blank calendar page or ruler and pen
* photos of things for which you are thankful
* glue
* stickers, markers or crayons (optional

What to Do

1. Glue the blank calendar page to the poster board. If you don't have a ready made page you can make a calendar by making a grid with seven squares across and five down. Make each square 1½" x 1½". Number the squares to match the days of this month. If the current month is almost over, make the calendar for next month.

2. Decorate your poster board by gluing on pictures of things for which you are thankful. Add your own stickers or decorations to make your poster pretty.

3. Each day, write on the calendar what you are thankful for that day. No repeating!

4. At the end of the month, look back and see all the blessings God has given you. If you want to do another month, just glue a new calendar over the old one.

Tip #10

Persevere.

Persevere.

I can do everything through him who gives me strength.

~ **Philippians 4:13**

Faith watched as the pitcher released the ball. It was coming toward her. Faith swung the bat.

"Strike one," called the umpire.

Faith got ready for the second pitch. The pitcher let the ball fly. She swung.

"Strike two," called the umpire.

Faith gripped the bat and took her stance for the next pitch. The ball was released. She swung again.

"Strike three," called the umpire.

Faith dropped the bat in disgust. She plodded over to the bench and dropped onto it.

"I'm no good at this. I don't know why I signed up to play softball," Faith said to Livia, sitting next to her on the bench. "I wish I could play like you do."

"You wouldn't have said that if you'd seen me play last year," Livia said. "I was awful. If I could manage to hit the ball I was always out at first base. I was the slowest runner. And besides that, I couldn't catch worth anything either!"

"You're kidding!" Faith said. "But now you're the star of the team."

"That's because my older brothers wouldn't let me give up after last season. They made me go out and practice an hour a night," Livia said. "They pitched to me, coached me on batting, taught me to throw, had me catch balls, and made me run a zillion sprints. I could play in my sleep!"

"Well all that practice sure paid off," Faith said. "Do you think you could teach me what your brothers taught you?"

"Sure," Livia said. "We'll start tonight — and I'm sure my brothers would love to have someone new to torture!"

When something gets difficult you may feel like quitting. It's hard to keep trying and failing. If Livia had given up, she would never have become the star of the baseball team. You might be surprised what you can do if you persevere. And if Faith practices consistently, she will improve. She may never be the star, but she will get better.

WHAT IS PERSEVERANCE?

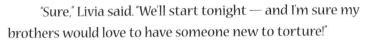

"Perseverance" means to keep going and keep trying in spite of difficulty or discouragement. That's hard to do. Sometimes it's easier to give up.

The Apostle Paul is a good example of someone who persevered. In Philippians 3:13-14 he says, "Brothers, I do not consider myself yet to have taken hold of it. But one thing I do: Forgetting what is behind and straining toward what is ahead, I press on toward the goal to win the prize for which God has called me heavenward in Christ Jesus."

Paul had a goal in mind: to take the gospel of Christ to those who needed to hear it. Do you think it was easy for him to reach that goal? No. In 2 Corinthians 11:23-27, Paul explains, "I have worked much harder, been in prison more frequently, been flogged more severely, and been exposed to death again and again. Five times I received from the Jews the forty lashes minus one. Three times I was beaten with rods, once I was stoned, three times I was shipwrecked, I spent a night and a day in the open sea, I have been constantly on the move. I have been in danger from rivers, in danger from bandits, in danger from my own countrymen, in danger from Gentiles; in danger in the city, in danger in the country, in danger at sea; and in danger from false brothers, I have labored and toiled and have often gone without sleep; I have known hunger and thirst and have often gone without food; I have been cold and naked."

TiNY Tip! Before giving up, practice 10 minutes a night and see how you progress by the end of the week.

Did Paul have good reason to give up? Yes! But he didn't, and because he didn't, many churches were started and many people became Christians. And during all of that, Paul wrote several long letters to different churches with advice on living the Christian life and how to run a church. Those letters became part of the New Testament. Their advice is still good for us today!

A Shining Example

Do you have a lamp? Have you listened to recorded music? Have you ever watched a movie? If you have, then you've benefited from the perseverance of one man: Thomas Edison.

Edison was the youngest of seven children. He only went to school for three months, but his mother taught him at home and he also learned a lot from reading books on his own. Not even going deaf at age 12 stopped him from learning and experimenting. Edison had over 1,000 patented inventions, but he is best known for the light bulb. It's easy to take that invention for granted, but the next time you turn on your light, remind yourself that it took Edison 9,990 separate experiments to come up with a light bulb that would work.

It seems like Edison would have gotten discouraged with so many failures, but he didn't. After failing 8,000 times to make a storage battery he said, "Well, at least we know 8,000 things don't work." Inventing wasn't easy but he persevered until he got it right.

LiFE QUiZ! Do You Have Perseverance?

Do you hang in there or do you bail out when things get tough? Take the quiz below. Be honest about which choice you would really make.

1. You are doing a science project about pulleys. It's the night before it's due and you just can't get it to work right. You:

a. Decide not to turn it in.

b. Ask a parent to give you some ideas about what could be wrong and how you could fix it.

c. Rig it so that it looks like it will work, write a good report to go with it and hope the teacher doesn't test it.

2. Your track coach wants you to do the high jump. No matter what you do you knock the bar off at the same height every time? You:

a. Ask the coach to put you in long jump instead and move someone else to high jump.

b. Decide that's as high as you will ever jump and give up.

c. Ask your coach for some extra help in finding a way to make it over the bar.

3. You start a cross-stitched picture for your grandmother for her birthday. It's harder than you thought! It will take countless hours to finish. You:

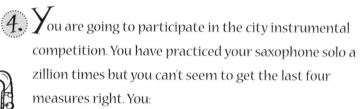

a. Ask your mom to do half of it and make the gift from both of you.

b. Ask your mom to show you how to make it easier, and keep working on it a little at a time.

c. Put it in a drawer to finish when you are older.

4. You are going to participate in the city instrumental competition. You have practiced your saxophone solo a zillion times but you can't seem to get the last four measures right. You:

a. Decide not to participate after all. There's always next year, and, after all, you are a beginner.

b. Play the last part really fast and hope no one notices the mistakes.

c. Ask your band director to go over it with you and then practice some more.

5. After watching a clown ride a unicycle at the circus you talk your parents into buying you a unicycle for your birthday. You soon realize that riding the unicycle isn't nearly as easy as it looked. You:

a. Practice a little every day until you can do it.

b. Give the unicycle to your little brother. He thinks it's neat.

c. Sell the unicycle at your family's yard sale and give the money to missions.

Score yourself and see how you did.

1. a. 0 points for not finishing.

b. 3 points for sticking with it and getting help.

c. No credit for rigging up the project.

2. a. 1 point for choosing something else rather than quitting the team.

b. 0 points for quitting. If it really is your best, accept it but don't quit.

c. 3 points for getting help and hanging in there.

3. a. 1 point for wanting to finish even if you need help.

b. 3 points for finishing it yourself even though it takes a long time.

c. 0 points for giving up.

4. a. 0 points for not trying.

b. 1 point for trying even though you didn't give it your best.

c. 3 points for practicing until you get it right.

5. **a.** 3 points for working at it until you can ride it.
b. 1 point for giving it to your brother.
c. 1 point for thinking of missions.

Total: _____

12-15: You are doing a great job at persevering even when things get hard.

8-11: Not too bad, just try sticking with some projects to make them work.

7 or less: You are falling short of perseverance. Read on for some ideas that will help you practice perseverance.

You can practice perseverance in your daily life, just as the girls below did.

PERSEVERANCE AT SCHOOL

Giving up may seem easier at times, but then you miss the satisfaction of overcoming an obstacle or solving a problem. Here are some ways that other girls have shown perseverance.

Chimeka wanted to make the track team but she wasn't fast enough. Also, she felt sluggish from eating fat-filled snacks after school. Chimeka decided that she really wanted to be on the team, so she made a plan. The first thing she did was ask her mother to buy fruit and cheese for after-school snacks rather than greasy potato chips. Then each day she spent recess running. If she couldn't get friends to run with her, she ran alone. By track season she wasn't super speedy, but she had built up a lot of endurance, and that got her a place on the team.

What good choices did Chimeka make?

_____

After she made her plan, do you think Chimeka ever got discouraged? If so, in what ways?

_____

_____

How did her perseverance help her?

_____

_____

Haley wanted to win the school spelling bee and go on to the city competition. But when she looked at the long list of words she needed to memorize, Haley wasn't sure she could do it. So she broke the list into parts and worked on one part a day until she had memorized the whole list.

Haley won the school competition and went on the city championship. She placed tenth in the city competition, so she plans to work harder next year so she will have an ever better chance at winning. Now she knows that she can do it if she works at it every day.

How did Haley feel when she first saw the list of words?

_____

What was her plan for accomplishing her goal?

_____

_____

Danielle was on the YMCA swimming team. She was a fast swimmer, but she wasn't quick off the start block. The slow start added several seconds to her time.

Danielle disliked starting on the blocks because she was afraid she'd fall in before the start gun sounded, or that she'd lose her goggles when she hit the water. So she asked the coach to give her extra help to overcome her fears. After several practice sessions, Danielle began shaving seconds off of her times because of her increased speed in leaving the start block.

What good choices did Danielle make?

_____

How did perseverance help her?

_____

In what area do you need to show perseverance?

_____

What kind of plan will you make to persevere?

_____

_____

PRACTICING PERSEVERANCE

Feel like giving up? Try some of the ideas below, or some of your own.

Ask for help. Can't do your math? Can't do a cartwheel? Ask for help from someone who can. A friend, teacher or coach may have just the advice you need. Don't hesitate to get help when you need it. Someone else's input may mean the difference between success and failure!

Try a different approach. For example, if you can't memorize your spelling words by writing them five times like your teacher suggests, why not set them to music? Sing the letters to the tune of "Old McDonald Had a Farm." Or maybe you can spell the words with a rap beat. Whatever your situation might be, remember that there are many different ways to achieve the same goal. Be creative!

Practice. There are some people who can do just about anything on their first try. But most people have to practice if they want to excel. You might have to practice your saxophone solo three times a night for a month until you are comfortable with it, or you might need to do five handstands a night for weeks before you advance to the next gymnastics level. If you

make practice part of your daily routine, after a while it will be like brushing your teeth or taking a shower.

Be realistic. You may not be the choir's soloist but you might be a good alto. You might be a good outfielder but not the star of the team. Don't quit an activity or give up on a project because you aren't the very best or an award winner. You'll never

be happy if you always have to be first place. Have fun without being number one!

Finish your commitments.

If you agree to paint scenery for the play but find you don't like doing it and then quit, the scenery might not get done in time. Or if you've agreed to help with the toddlers at vacation Bible school but decide you don't enjoy toddlers, hang in there for the week anyway. You will learn something from every activity you do whether you like it or not, even if it's just what you do and don't like!

Tiny Tip! Need a little encouragement to try something difficult? Give yourself a sticker or star on a calendar for each day you try.

Pray.

Ask God to help you hang in there when you want to quit. He understands you better than anyone else because He made you.

WHEN IT'S OKAY TO QUIT

Is it always wrong to give up on something or to quit an activity? No. There are some good reasons to quit. Here are a few.

The class or sport **wasn't what you thought it would be.** Perhaps you joined your school's photography club thinking you would go on trips and take pictures. But after you joined, you found out the club is more about discussing cameras, dark room procedures and other technical topics for which you aren't ready. This is a time when it might be better to look for a less technical club or activity.

The **instructor or coach is abusive** or asks you to violate your values. If you feel a coach is going too far in yelling at you or your teammates, uses inappropriate language or in any way makes you uncomfortable, talk to your parents about it. If you cannot come up with a suitable solution, it's time to look for another activity.

You sincerely **lose interest** in an activity. You might have thought flag corps was really fun at first, but now you're tired of it. If you've completed the whole season, you might want to think about a new activity for the next year. But don't quit in the middle — finish your commitment!

The activity **interferes with family or church** activities. Maybe you think it would be fun to be on volleyball team, but after joining you find out you're required to practice almost every weeknight and that the games are going to be on Saturdays and Sundays. If you cannot do that and still have time for your family and church, you should reconsider being on the team. Talk with your parents about how much time is too much time to spend on an activity.

You practice and give an activity your best shot, but after trying for a good amount of time you still **cannot do it.** Remember, not everyone has the same abilities! The key is to find out what you can do and not dwell on what you can't do.

The activity is affecting you physically. **It hurts!** We're not talking about a few sore muscles here, but consistent pain. Sometimes bad knees and other problems can keep you from doing something that you really want to do. Find another activity!

WRAPPING IT UP

Learning to persevere is difficult, especially when something is hard to do! If you are in the habit of giving up when an activity becomes difficult, try to break the habit. Stick with it and you will be amazed at how much you can accomplish!

Memory Verse

Write the memory verse here and keep it in mind when you feel like quitting. Memorize it!

_____

_____

Jot It Down

What types of activities are most difficult for you?

_____

What do you do when you feel like giving up?

_____

_____

Tell about a time you persevered and accomplished something you didn't think you could do. How did you feel?

_____

_____

Get Crafty! Perseverance Pals

The caterpillar is a good example to us. After it eats, it works to build a cocoon and stays in it until it is transformed into a beautiful butterfly. When it becomes a butterfly, it breaks free and flies! That's like God's work in us. When we persevere and do the things He wants us to do, we are transformed into the people He wants us to be. We become beautiful butterflies for God!

Make these refrigerator magnets to remind you to persevere for God as He shapes you into one of His butterflies.

What You Need

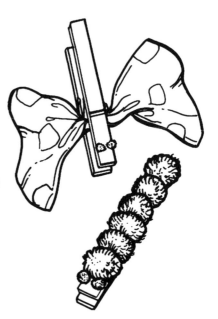

❋ two spring-type clothespins

❋ four small pom-poms

❋ four wiggle eyes (available at craft stores, or use mini pom-poms)

❋ 3" piece of chenille wire (pipe cleaner)

❋ tissue paper

❋ glue

❋ self-stick magnets

What to Do

Caterpillar

1. Coat one side of a clothespin with glue.

2. Press pom-poms on the clothespin in a row.

3. Glue eyes on the pom-pom that is on the closed end of the clothespin.

4. Attach a magnet to the back of the clothespin and stick your caterpillar on the refrigerator.

Butterfly

1. Select tissue paper in your favorite colors. You will need one 6" x 8" piece for the body (or an 8" x 10" piece if you want a bigger butterfly) and smaller pieces for decoration.

2. Decorate the butterfly's wings by gluing small pieces of tissue paper on the larger piece. Design them in any pattern you like.

3. After the tissue has dried, gather it in the center and slide it between the clamps of the clothespin.

4. Place the piece of chenille wire between the clamps also. Turn up the ends for antennae.

5. Glue eyes on the top of the clothespin near the front.

6. Fasten a magnet to the back of the clothespin and stick your new magnet on the refrigerator.

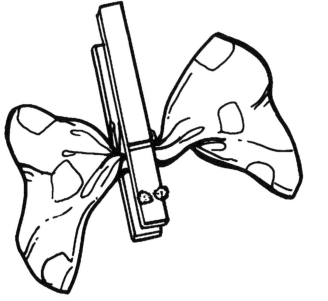

Tip #11

Guard your tongue.

Do not let any unwholesome talk come out of your mouths, but only what is helpful for building others up according to their needs, that it may benefit those who listen.

~ Ephesians 4:29

"You should visit my church," Victoria told her friend Shay as they stood in the school lunch line. "We have a great youth group. We have parties and go on camping trips and all kinds of stuff."

"I don't know," Shay said. "I'm not really a religious person."

"You don't have to be religious, just come with me sometime," said Victoria. She picked up her tray and turned to go to her table. Suddenly a boy bumped into Victoria, causing her to stumble into Shay.

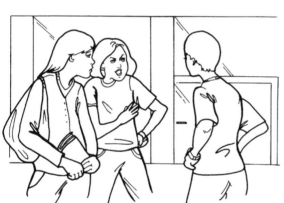

"I... I... uh... I'm sorry," the boy, a special ed. student, stammered.

"Watch where you're going, jerk! You almost made me fall!" Victoria lashed out. "I wish you retards could eat in your own room so we wouldn't have to put up with you!"

"Victoria, lay off him. It was an accident," Shay said calmly, leading the way to a table.

Victoria set her tray down. "Why don't those weird kids eat in their own classroom? They're gross, and they're always in the way. They give me the creeps!"

"One of my cousins has Down's Syndrome and she's really sweet. She just doesn't understand everything," Shay said. "You shouldn't have said all those things to that boy. He has feelings, you know."

"Feelings, but no brain!" Victoria said as she opened her milk.

Shay put down her slice of pizza. "Hey, I'm not the religious one here but I don't talk about him like that. Doesn't your church teach you about being nice?"

Tongues!

Has your tongue (what you say) ever gotten you into trouble? It can do that! James, who wrote the book of James in the Bible, spends almost a whole chapter talking about the tongue. He says, "With the tongue we praise our Lord and Father, and with it we curse men, who have been made in God's likeness. Out of the same mouth come praise and cursing. My brothers, this should not be" (James 3:9-10). Would that be a good passage for Victoria to remember? How about you?

Tiny Tip! if someone puts you down, surprise him or her by answering with a compliment!

The way you talk when you are with your Sunday school teacher or in church should be the same way you talk all week at school with your friends or even those you don't know or like. It should also be how you talk when you are at home with pesky little brothers or snobby older sisters. There are both good ways to use your tongue and bad ways to use your tongue.

What are some good ways to use your tongue?

_____

What are some bad uses of the tongue?

_____

TWISTED TONGUES

Read the following stories and see if you can identify the twisted ways these girls used their tongues.

Michelle waited anxiously as her teacher handed back the math test. She hadn't studied as much as she should have. She'd planned to study, but there were too many other fun things to do and math just wasn't that interesting to her. Formulas and fractions couldn't compete with computer games and television.

Mr. Ray approached Michelle's desk and laid her test, face down, on the desk. Michelle lifted up a corner and peeked: 55%. An F! Michelle quickly stuffed the test into her notebook.

"What did you get on the test?" her friend Carrie asked. "I got an 88%."

"Really? Me too," Michelle said.

How did Michelle use words in a wrong way?

_____

What could she have said instead?

_____

If you said that Michelle lied, you were right. Look up Proverbs 12:22 in your Bible and write how it says God feels about lies.

_____

_____

Is lying ever right? No. Even though you know that, you still may be tempted to lie at times. There are several reasons you might lie. Here are some of them:

You fear punishment. Whether you broke your mom's favorite cup or you didn't get home on time – sometimes it seems easier to make up a lie than to confess the truth.

You don't like your parents' rules. Maybe your parents say you can't go to the mall with a friend or that you can't have a friend over while your parents aren't home. You don't like the rule so you break it and then lie about it.

You want to impress others. Everyone but you seems to have a billion things they are good at, right? You wrongly think your talents and accomplishments don't match up to theirs, so you invent a few.

You want to fit in. Perhaps your friends don't go to church and you're afraid they'll make fun of you if they find out you do. So you say, "Me? Church? You've got to be kidding!"

Is lying really that bad? Yes. Here are some things that happen when you lie:

Others lose their trust in you.

You lose your integrity.

You get hurt.

Others get hurt.

Your Christian testimony is blown.

Sam walked into school. She saw Jill, a new girl, walking to her locker. Sam walked over to Jill.

"Did you forget to brush your hair this morning or did you use the toilet brush?" Sam asked.

The other students nearby laughed. Jill blushed.

"Did you get your clothes at Goodwill or are those the clothes they wouldn't take?" Sam continued in a taunting tone.

"Good one, Sam!" a boy called out.

The other students laughed, but Jill wanted to cry. She knew Sam was just getting started. She was used to it. It had been like this every day since she'd moved to this town and started this school.

Even worse, Sam was in her Sunday school class! Of course, Sam didn't say those things to Jill in front of the Sunday school teacher. When Mrs. Graham was around, Sam was a perfect angel, quoting Scripture and offering to pray. Jill wished Sam would act like a Christian all of the time and not just in Sunday school.

How is Sam using her words in the wrong way?

_____

How do you talk at church?

_____

How do you talk at school?

_____

Look up Colossians 4:6. How does Paul say we should always speak?

_____

Slams, cutdowns, putdowns. No matter what you call them, they're all wrong! Sometimes they might be funny, but not when you're the target. They shouldn't be funny when other people are the targets either.

Mean criticisms are used to make others look bad. It only takes a few well-placed words to hurt someone. It might even happen unintentionally. A "slam" made in fun may hit too close to the truth and hurt someone's feelings. The worse part is, you may not realize it. That person might slam you right back while yours is hurting him. Little darts of words tossed back and forth can leave a bad sting.

What can you do if someone starts slamming another person?

_____

"Did you hear what Karen did?" Melissa asked the group of girls gathered around her locker.

"No, what?" Anne asked.

"Well, I heard that she cheated on the achievement tests last week and she got suspended. That's why she's not here today," Melissa said gleefully.

"Really? Wow! I wonder if she'll have to take fifth grade over again," Megan said.

"Who has to take fifth grade over again?" Paul asked as he joined the group.

"Karen might have to take fifth grade over again for cheating on the achievement tests last week," Anne said.

The bell rang and the students hurried off to their classroom.

"I have some news," Mr. Peters said to the class. "It's about one of your classmates who isn't here today."

Anne and Melissa exchanged knowing looks. "Told you so," Melissa mouthed.

"One of our students, Karen, scored so well on her achievement tests that she might be invited to take part in a summer program for gifted students. Today she is having an interview with a panel of teachers who will decide who is accepted into the program. I think it's very exciting to have one of our own students considered for the program, and I'm sure we all wish her good luck. Now take out last night's homework and pass it forward. Melissa, please collect the papers from each row."

Melissa wanted to slide down in her chair to avoid the accusing looks of classmates who'd heard what she'd said about Karen. Now she had to walk in front of the class and collect their papers.

In what wrong way did Melissa use her tongue?

If you said Melissa was gossiping, you're right! Gossip is any information you pass along that shouldn't be shared with others except by the person involved. Sometimes gossip is true and sometimes it isn't. Often times gossip involves someone making a guess about a situation without really knowing the facts, like Melissa did.

Look up Proverbs 11:13 in your Bible. What does it say that people who gossip do?

_____

How do they do it?

_____

What should Melissa have done before sharing her story about Karen with everyone?

_____

What should she do now?

_____

When others hear you gossip, they may listen and enjoy your stories, but you might find that they are also cautious around you. They don't want to be the next target of your gossip! Think about something that no one knows about you except yourself. Would you want this story shared around school or church? It's a good strategy to stop and think about other's feelings before spreading gossip.

"Oh, I am so mad," Becca spewed at Cole, a classmate. "I can't believe you forgot to do your part of our history project! You idiot! Now what am I going to do? I'm never speaking to you again!"

Becca grabbed her books and stomped off to class. She felt anger boiling up inside of her. She'd like to punch Cole right in the nose!

What kind of words is Becca using?

_____

What advice does James 1:19 offer from which Becca could benefit?

_____

When you get angry, you might find harsh, angry words coming out of your mouth before you even know it! Words are powerful. They can build someone up, but they can also destroy. Angry words almost always do harm.

How can you avoid angry words? Here are some ideas.

Pray and ask God to calm you down.

Stop and count to 10. It really works!

Walk away from the situation until you are calm enough to deal with it without anger.

Write in a journal or talk to a trusted adult about what made you angry.

Burn off your anger by running, biking or in-line skating.

Think about the real problem and not the person who might have caused it. How can you fix the problem?

What can you do when you feel like lashing out at someone in anger?

_____

_____

*T*amra crouched low as she sped along on her in-line skates. A sharp curve was coming up and she didn't want to miss it. As she leaned into a curve, one of her blades hit a pebble. Tamra lost her balance and tumbled onto the cement. She muttered a swear word.

"I can't believe you said that word," Gabi said. "If my parents ever heard me say that I'd be grounded for a year!"

"My parents never hear me say any cuss words," Tamra said.

"But what about God? Remember last week when Miss Simmons read those verses in Sunday school about God being everywhere and knowing everything?" Gabi reminded her.

"Do you really think God has time to sit around and worry about whether I cuss or not?" Tamra said, justifyingly. "Besides, if I hadn't been wearing my knee and elbow pads I'd really be hurt!"

In what wrong way was Tamra using her tongue?

_____

Look up Ephesians 5:4 in your Bible. What does it say about your language?

_____

When you fall into the habit of using swear words, you discredit your Christian testimony. Other students may think you are not much different than they are.

One type of swearing is using God's name when you are angry or even just talking. What does the Bible say about using God's name as a swear word? Look in Exodus 20:7 and Deuteronomy 5:11 and write your answer.

_____

_____

Lying, slamming, gossiping, using angry words and swearing are all wrong uses of the tongue. If you've gotten into the habit of using your tongue these ways, now is the time to break the habit. Stop and think before you talk!

REAL Girls

TAME TONGUES

Just as there are wrong ways to use the tongue, there are also good uses for your words. One of those good uses is sharing your faith. Here are some ways other girls do that each day.

Annie B. of Lake Charles, Louisiana, shares her faith by singing. She is part of a church group that sings in local nursing homes once a month. She also sings in a youth choir and she sometimes sings in a youth quartet that provides special music during the church service.

Mikala S. is part of a prayer group that meets before school twice a week in Omaha, Nebraska, to pray for teachers and students.

Meaghan F. speaks out against drugs and alcohol in Laurel, Mississippi. She tells other students that drugs and alcohol will ruin their lives but that God has a plan for them. She helps those around her understand why drugs are bad by telling about her brother who had a drug habit but is now drug-free.

Kelli R. of New York City shares her faith anytime she has to do an oral report. If she has to do a book report, she reports on a Christian adventure or mystery book or a missionary biography. She carefully selects Christian books that the kids in her class might like, such as fiction and mysteries.

These are just a few ways that others share their faith. Which of these would you like to do or in what other ways could you use your words to share your faith?

___

Encouraging others is also a good use of the tongue and it doesn't require a lot of time or money. Encouragement can be very simple, as these girls have found.

Jasmine Y. of Salisbury, North Carolina, tries to encourage others who aren't doing well at school by offering to help them and by telling them they will do better on their next test or report.

REAL Girls

Catherine U. of El Cajon, California, buys note cards and writes notes to different people each month. She has written to her Sunday school teacher, Bible club leader, pastor, parents, teachers, lunchroom workers, librarian and bus driver.

Janie L. is a cheerleader in Madison, Wisconsin. She encourages the players by cheering for them and also telling them they are doing a good job, whether the team wins or not. She makes posters and hangs them in the school hallways before every game.

Guard Your Tongue.

Shelby G. of St. Cloud, Minnesota, writes a newsletter about her church's youth activities. She mails the newsletter to missionary kids once a month to let them know they aren't forgotten while they're overseas.

Which of these would you like to do or what else could you do to encourage those around you?

_____

_____

Here are some more ways to encourage others:

Tell your **Sunday school teacher** one thing that you liked about the lesson.

Talk to a **friend** about a problem she's having.

Take time to compliment three people today. Be sincere.

Tell a **classmate** that you'll help her study for her next math test so she'll do better.

Tell your **brother** he did a good job on his sports team.

Tell your **dad** that you appreciate his hard work.

P raising God is another good use of the tongue. If you have trouble thinking of things for which to praise God, try reading some of the Psalms aloud. Start with Psalms 9, 33 and 48.

You can write a psalm of your own. Just finish this sentence and add a few more.

I praise You, God, because You have:

_____

_____

Giving thanks is a good use of the tongue that everyone can do! Not only will others feel good when you thank them, you'll feel good, too. This week, get into a gratitude attitude by thanking each of the people on the list below. Check off each one as you do it. Add some of your own at the bottom!

_____ Thank your dad or mom for cooking a meal for you.

_____ Thank your dad or mom for doing your laundry.

_____ Thank your dad or mom for working hard to buy your food and clothes.

_____ Thank your Sunday school teacher for teaching you about God.

_____ Thank your pastor for teaching you about God.

_____ Thank a brother or sister for helping you with something.

_____ Thank a friend for listening to your problems.

_____ Thank a teacher for taking time to explain a hard concept.

_____ Thank your bus driver for getting you to school safely.

_____ Thank the school or church janitor for keeping the building clean.

_____ Thank the cafeteria workers for serving the food.

_____ Thank God for sending Jesus!

_____

_____

_____

_____

WRAPPING IT UP

Every day you use thousands of words. Are they good words that help and encourage others? Or are they harmful words that tear others down and destroy friendships? Stop and think before you speak this week. Ask God to let the words of your mouth be acceptable in his sight (Psalm 19:14).

Memory Verse

Write this chapter's memory verse below. Think about it often this week as you use your tongue for good.

_____

_____

Jot It Down

Do you use your words more often for good or for harm?

_____

What changes do you need to make?

_____

Are slams and gossip a big problem at your school? If so, what can you do to improve the situation?

_____

_____

Apple Mouths

You now know a lot about the bad and good uses of your mouth. It is easy to use your mouth in bad ways, such as gossip or taunting. But you can also do good with your mouth by encouraging others or praising God. Think about good ways to use your words as you make this fun, edible mouth.

What You Need

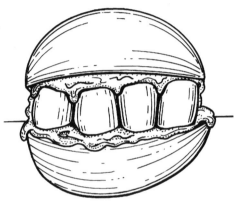

* large red apple
* miniature marshmallows
* peanut butter
* knife

What to Do

1. Wash the apple.

2. Have an adult help you slice the apple into eight slices. You will use two slices for each "mouth."

3. Place one side so the red part is facing you. Spread peanut butter on the fruit part. This is the bottom "lip" of your mouth.

4. Fit marshmallow "teeth" into the peanut butter.

5. Spread another apple slice with peanut butter as the top lip. Place this slice on the other side of the teeth.

6. Share your Apple Mouths with your family for a special snack.

Answers to Puzzles

Talent Crossword, pages 39-40

Across	Down
3. Moses	1. Peter
4. Shamgar	2. Boaz
6. Samson	3. Mary
8. Andrew	5. Gideon
10. David	7. Noah
11. Joshua	8. Adam
12. Solomon	9. Dorcas
13. Paul	11. Joseph

Secret Code, page 54

Whatever your hand finds to do, do it with all your might.

— Ecclesiastes 9:10

Set Priorities, pages 88-89

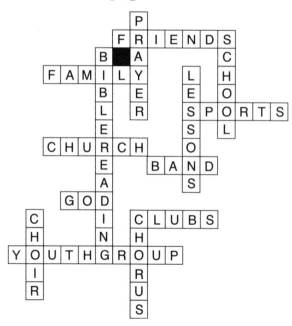

Dial-a-Message Puzzle, pages 140-141

Submit yourselves, then, to God. Resist the devil and he will flee from you.

— James 4:7

The fun devotional that helps girls grow closer to God.

God and Me! and *God and Me! 2* are packed with over 100 devotionals, plus memory verses, stories, journal space and fun activities to help you learn more about the Bible.

LP 46823
ISBN 1-885358-54-7

LP 46829
ISBN 1-58411-056-2

Attention: Christian babysitters!

This is the only manual you will need to be the best babysitter on the block. *The Official Christian Babysitting Guide* has everything you want to know about taking care of kids. Plus, get ideas for keeping kids busy with lots of Bible crafts, games, snacks and songs. Most importantly, you will find Scriptures and strategies for serving God as you serve families. Get it today and find out how you can be a blessing as you babysit!

LP 48021
ISBN 1-58411-027-9

Get them at your favorite Christian bookstore!